SPIRES THAT ASPIRE TO INSPIRE

St. Ignatius Church

*A history of St. Ignatius Church,
a San Francisco Landmark*

PETER MERLE DEVINE

Palmetto Publishing Group
Charleston, SC

Spires That Aspire to Inspire – St. Ignatius Church

First Edition

Printed in the United States

ISBN-13: 978-1-64111-307-6
ISBN-10: 1-64111-307-3

CONTENTS

DEDICATION

This history of St. Ignatius Church relies on the memoirs of many Jesuit priests dating back to their first arrival in Northwest in the 1840s. However, the primary sources for this book are from four great historical works. Father John McGloin, SJ, a master historian of early California history, completed his academic career with a comprehensive volume entitled *Jesuits by the Golden Gate*, published by the University of San Francisco in 1972. One of his master's degree students, Father Terrance Mahan, SJ, completed his dissertation under Father McGloin's supervision, the unpublished *History of St. Ignatius Church (1951)*, the first work to focus exclusively on the church. Two laymen wrote histories of their respective schools in 2005 to celebrate their 150th anniversary: Paul Totah, *Spiritus Magis: 150 years of St. Ignatius College Prep*, published by the high school, and Alan Ziajka, *Legacy and Promise*, published by the university.

St. Ignatius owes its legacy and legend to many great Jesuit leaders from Father Maraschi in 1855 to Father William Dunne in the 1930s to Father Charles Dullea, SJ in the 1960s, and Brother Manuel Silvera, SJ and all the Jesuit priests and brothers throughout this history. Several modern Jesuits standout, including the curators Father James Blaettler and Father John Lucas, as well as award-winning designer Joel Villanon and Ray Frost sacristan and archivist, all of whom have maintained the artistic beauty of the church into this millenium. This manuscript benefitted from many eyes and ears who guided its accuracy and design, especially Charles A. Fracchia, noted San Francisco historian, Robert Vergara, history teacher at St. Ignatius

College Prep, Lorraine Scullion and Mark Diamond (who initiated the project with Fr. Greg Bonfiglio).

We dedicate this volume to two Jesuit leaders who stand out as the pioneer pastors of the modern St. Ignatius Parish – Father Charles Gagan, SJ, and Father Gregory Bonfiglio, SJ. They have created the Second Century St. Ignatius as an architectural wonder and as a living faith community – two Jesuit priests who aspire to inspire with their vision for the future and a reverence for the past.

Built on the shoulders of the Western Province of the Society of Jesus and local civic leaders, this iconic historic structure is the fifth home of the St. Ignatius community. Both the historical and current faith communities of the St. Ignatius Parish are the heartbeat to its history and future. St. Ignatius Parish attracts thousands of visitors annually, and this historic landmark also serves as home to a vibrant parish community. Generations have come to St. Ignatius for weddings, baptisms, funerals, graduations, concerts, and other community events. We preserve the history of this story to inspire the next generations to continue to build on the legacy and promise, the Spiritus Magis, of the Jesuits by the Golden Gate.

1. *Spiritus Magis: 150 years of St. Ignatius College Preparatory* by Paul Totah St. Ignatius College Prep 2005

2. *Jesuits by the Golden Gate* by Rev. John McGloin, SJ University of San Francisco 1972

3. *Legacy and Promise* by Alan Ziajka University of San Francisco 2005

4. *History of St. Ignatius Church*, unpublished dissertation by Rev. Terrence Mahan, SJ 1951

PRELUDE:

Elsie Robinson, in a 1914 national column for the Hearst papers, wrote "Listen World":

I look across a deep valley and other hills to one which tops them all and there, tall and gleaming in beauty, rise the spires of St. Ignatius .... a symbol of all that is best and bravest in the city life.

Before they were built the hill on which they stand was merely sand dunes ... {as} the city began to spread, and the vision of men spread with it. And out of that vision came these lovely spires.

When the great storms sweep out of the Pacific, darkening the town, or the fog veils the valley in blue mist, I like to look toward those gleaming spires which seem to float in another world.

ST. IGNATIUS TOWERS OVER THE BAY, THE GOLDEN GATE, AND THE PACIFIC WITH TWIN SPIRES THAT INSPIRE AND ASPIRE.

ST. IGNATIUS CHURCH – THE HEART OF SAN FRANCISCO

Chapter One

BY CHANCE AND ACCIDENT

By chance and by accident, on January 24, 1848 James Marshall spotted something sparkling in the saw mill's run-off water: gold. James Sutter, owner and boss, ordered absolute secrecy from his employees. As with most "secrets," news spread quickly from the American River community to the sleepy pueblo by the bay, then like wildfire to the world. Between January 1848 and December 1849, the population of sleepy Yerba Buena increased from 1,000 to over 25,000, a group of immigrants affectionately known as the 49ers. Yerba Buena quickly developed into a wild frontier town, took on the name of the patron saint of Mission Saint Francis of Assisi, then became a major metropolitan center of commerce and trade. From its many hilltops to its filled-in marshlands, the entrance of the Pacific drew people from New York, Chicago, St. Louis, as well as England, France, Italy, Spain, and Argentina, Brazil, and Mexico. For the Chinese, California became known as Gold Mountain.

Even before gold was discovered, the members of the Society of Jesus, the Jesuits, arrived in the American Northwest during the

1840s. Under the pioneer leadership of Father Peter De Smet, SJ, the Jesuits established missions in the Oregon territory, working with a growing community of farmers and the native peoples. From 1844 until 1848, the Northwest missions thrived; a call went out to Rome, and more Italian Jesuit missionaries soon arrived to minister to the growing needs of the frontier communities. However, Father John Roothaan, Superior General of the Jesuits in Rome, warned these missionaries not to scatter their resources, not to expand into lower Oregon or Northern California.

Gold Fever infected Oregon, and farmers left their crops and herds to seek their fortunes along the American River. The Jesuits' congregations almost completely relocated to the Sierra foothills. The Oregonian Jesuits wondered if they should follow their flocks. Before they could write Rome for permission, two Oregonian Jesuit priests -- Father Michael Acolti,SJ and Father John Nobili, SJ -- received a letter from two French priests in San Francisco. The priests complained they were overwhelmed with a flood of Catholics landing on the shores of San Francisco Bay from Europe and South America. They begged the Jesuits to send priests. Rather than await permission from Rome, which could take close to half a year, Fathers Acolti and Nobili discerned it wiser to seek approval from the local authority, the northwestern Jesuit superior, Father Joseph Joset.

In his letter Father Acolti contended that circumstances had changed and permission from Rome no longer applied. His passionate pleas wore Father Joset down, and in November 1849 the superior reluctantly agreed the two Jesuits could set sail for San Francisco. The two "49er" Jesuit arrived in San Francisco on December 8 – the feast of the Immaculate Conception. Their original plan included serving both in the city and in the Sierra foothills. However, they quickly discovered only one other priest now resided in San Francisco while 23 separate Protestant congregations had ministers, so they decided their fortunes lay in the city not the gold mines.

Father Accolti's letter to Rome ("A Memorial of the Journey to California") aptly captures the wildness of the gold rush town: "We were able to set foot on the longed-for shores of what goes under the name of San Francisco, but which, whether it should be called a mad house or Babylon, I am at a loss to determine." He further went on to describe the "open immorality, the reign of crime which, brazen faced, triumphed." So he and Father Nobili discerned the city would be fertile ground for their priestly work.

The move to San Francisco involved another change: they were no longer under the authority of their Northwest bishop. Permission to administer the sacraments had to come from the Franciscan Minister of California stationed at Mission Santa Barbara, Father Jose Marie de Jesus Gonzales de Rubio. He wholeheartedly supported their mission in his letter of February 1, 1850, and in another letter on March 5th added a surprising request: He commissioned them to establish two Jesuit schools, called collegios (for students ages 6 – 18). Fathers Acolti and Nobili decided to split their ministry between two cities, San Francisco and San Jose, while they awaited approval for the founding of a collegio in San Jose from Father Superior General in Rome. On May 13, 1850, approval from Father General in Rome arrived, and Father Nobili became assistant pastor in Pueblo San Jose, the new state capital.

Newly appointed Joseph Alemany, Bishop of Monterey, took an immediate liking to Father Nobili and commissioned him as pastor of the first Jesuit parish in California, Mission Santa Clara in 1851. He also gave permission to establish the first Jesuit school at the Mission. That original Jesuit parish is still thriving, and the collegio became Bellarmine College Preparatory and the University of Santa Clara, home to the mission parish in the heart of Silicon Valley.

A SAD ACCIDENT – 1ST JESUIT SCHOOL IN SAN FRANCISCO SWEPT AWAY IN DEBT AND THE SAND DUNES.

In 1853, Fr. Flavian Fontaine, of the Congregation of the Sacred Hearts of Jesus and Mary, decided to build a college of Mission Dolores at 14th and Waller Streets; but after accruing over $2000 in debts, he fled to Panama. Father Nobili immediately saw this financial accident as an opportunity and asked Bishop Alemany for permission to purchase the property and open a school, even though there would not be a Jesuit parish attached. The purchase price from the creditors mushroomed to over $11,000, and the single teacher/principal Father Francis Veyret opened the first Jesuit school in San Francisco in 1854.

However, by September 1854, a few short months after opening, the school failed. The location lay too far to the western edge of the town and required travel over too many walk ways and sand dunes. In his comprehensive history of Saint Ignatius College Prep, *Spiritus Magis*, Paul Totah nicknames this school as the "College of Sorrows," both because of its history and its association with Mission Dolores.

TURIN JESUITS TURN THE TIDE -- FIRST ST. IGNATIUS CHURCH – JULY 15, 1855

SAN FRANCISCO - 1855

Good fortune would prevail for the Jesuits in San Francisco when the newly elected Jesuit Superior General, Father Peter Becks, designated California as mission territory for the province of Turin, Italy. Immediately the Turin provincial assigned more Jesuits to California, especially providential was the appointment of Father Anthony Maraschi, SJ to San Francisco.

Anthony Maraschi, born in the province of Piedmont, Italy in 1820, entered the Society of Jesus in 1841, then taught as a scholastic in Nice, then was ordained in 1949 in Marseilles before being assigned to Holy Cross College in Massachusetts where he taught Spanish and philosophy. Soon after he was assigned to Loyola

College in Maryland; after taking his final vows in 1854, he was "missioned" to San Francisco.

The San Francisco he encountered was not the thriving Gold Rush City of 1849, but a city in the midst of an economic depression. Once the mines "panned out," unemployment plagued the city. Over one third of San Francisco's retail stores were vacant. Undaunted, Father Maraschi served at St. Francis parish in North Beach, then St. Patrick's Parish at 3rd and Mission Street while scouting out a site for a Jesuit Church and college. Father Maraschi saw the possibility of the Jesuits having their own parish and *collegio* in San Francisco. Historian Paul Totah reports that Alemany "worried that the Jesuits, with the penchant for preaching, would lure away parishioners and their offerings from the archdiocesan churches." After the archbishop vetoed numerous possible properties as "too close to his Cathedral," finally he "pointed with a pen on the map" to a plot of land on the far outskirts of the city – the sand dunes of St. Ann's Valley between present day 4th and 5th Streets on Market Street, the southern side of the Powell and Market intersection.

Despite the isolated site, Father Maraschi predicted the Jesuits would not have to go to the city, the city would come to St Ignatius. Father Maraschi prophetically wrote in his memories, "Here, in time, will be the heart of a great city." This began the first of many historical "accidents" where the Jesuits of San Francisco proved to be not only great educators, but great real estate men.

Due to the long transit time for permissions to arrive from Father General in Rome, often the California Jesuits "anticipated permission." Father Maraschi perceived events and pastoral needs in San Francisco changing too quickly for the long wait. As a Jesuit historian once quipped: the California schools were founded on disobedience and run on disobedience, then most obediently blessed in hindsight.

When Father General in Rome officially recognized St. Ignatius Academy, Father Maraschi filed for incorporation under California law; the newly named St. Ignatius College could grant college degrees. Since faculty size was still limited, Father Maraschi himself taught Latin, Greek and Spanish, and served as the pastor, chief preacher, and building superintendent. He supervised church repairs and additions while also serving as the chief accountant not only for the parish and college, but the entire California and Oregon mission provinces. His hard work and dedication was celebrated in the *Alta California* newspaper in 1859 when they commended him "as a finished scholar and a man of high moral character … {who} labored incessantly to advance the interests of those under his care."

Even though he retired from the presidency of the college in 1862, he continued to serve as school treasurer. Alan Ziajka, USF historian in his history of USF entitled *Legacy & Promise*, notes that

Maraschi's first task was to raise the funds for the new church and classroom building. In addition to raising donations, he also received an unusual bequest of land near Point San Pablo in the East Bay, land that came to be known as "Maraschi's Ranch." Maraschi lived beyond the life span of the first and second campuses; his fundraising, and the sale of the ranch, eventually eliminated the entire debt of close of 1 million dollars. When he died in 1897, the City lost its first "Jesuit founding father." The church was packed with 49er families and thirty years of graduates from the college who came to celebrate the courage and perseverance of what San Francisco papers called "this pioneer priest."

Since the archbishop insisted the Jesuits not take up any collections to fund their venture (to avoid competition with neighboring parishes), Father Maraschi purchased the property for $11,500 from Thomas Larkin by borrowing the entire cost at 1.5% monthly interest, the beginning of the Jesuit indebtedness. The simple wooden structure, the first St. Ignatius Church, was dedicated by Bishop Alemany on July 15, 1855, and St. Ignatius Academy opened its doors to 3 students on October 15th. Richard McCabe and his two classmates were greeted by three faculty members – Father Maraschi, Father Bixio, and the first lay teacher Mr. John Haley. Enrollment grew slowly, increasing to 65 students by 1858.

Father Maraschi had courageously taken on a major indebtedness. If one converts the $11,500 price for the land and the $4,000 construction costs to 2018 dollars, the little Italian Jesuit took on a debt of $448,910. When the property eventually sold for far more, Maraschi was hailed as a real estate genius.

In 1930 the Society of California Pioneers dedicated the above plaque to commemorate the first campus in the Emporium Department Store. Now it hangs in the San Francisco Center on Market and Fifth.

For the first several years, the *collegio* and the parish fortunes shifted as much as the sand dunes surrounding them. The city experienced several earthquakes, major fires, crime, two different vigilante committees, and financial hardships; and the rains throughout the winter months made travel over the sand difficult. Nevertheless, the sand dune parish began to thrive. As Father Antoine Langlois wrote when he first visited the city, "in spite of the barrooms and saloons on every hand for the multitudes who wanted to frequent them … it was possible for a person to save his soul in San Francisco."

With the discovery of silver in Virginia City, the Nevada Comstock Lode created a second economic boom. The center of business shifted from Portsmouth Square to Market Street, and by 1861 Market Street was graded and paved. St. Ignatius Church and College was now – as Father Marschi predicted – located right in the center of the city. Sunday congregations increased to overflowing crowds due to the Jesuit's reputation as outstanding preachers; soon enrollments increased beyond the capacity of the one room school building. Father Maraschi and the Jesuit community discerned it was time to expand.

JUNE 30, 1863
SECOND RED BRICK ST. IGNATIUS – BUT POPULARITY "UNPARISHES" NEW SI

As founding pastor, Father Maraschi served for two years, then became the head of school. The second pastor Father Nicholas Congiato, appointed in 1857, served until 1863, the last pastor for the next 131 years.

The noted Native American Jesuit Father James Bouchard, a master preacher from St. Louis, packed the church for series of special missions. The overflowing crowds made the need for a larger church clearly evident. In 1862, Father Maraschi took on more debt to purchase the adjacent sand dunes and commissioned a 500-seat brick church; he also planned for a two-story classroom building for the expanding elementary, high school and college divisions. Tuition: $ 3 for the middle school preparatory, $5 for the larger high school, and $8 for the "high" collegiate classes. Enrollment grew to 550 students in only eight years.

One day while out for his daily stroll, Maraschi came across a very large bell that the fire department had ordered from England. It was manufactured by Naylor, Bickes and Company in Sheffield, England, and was at the time – 1859 – the largest bell ever made in England. It weighs 5, 825 (3 tons), is 5 feet 3 inches high with a diameter of 6 feet 2 inches. Since the bell itself was so heavy, it does not move -- the 4-foot 2-inch clapper moves to strike the tone. The windjammer named "The San Francisco" carted it to the city, but the Fire Department could no longer afford to pay the bill. After a few minutes of good old-fashioned Italian haggling, Maraschi decided to go $1300 more in debt – his new brick church needed a bell to call Catholics to Mass.

Popularity did come at a price: Father Maraschi had to take out additional loans to fund the expansion. But far more costly was the archbishop's decision to "unparish" St. Ignatius because the Jesuits were drawing crowds – and collections – from the neighboring parishes. Therefore, in a dispute over the deed to the property under conflicting canon laws, Archbishop Alemany removed St. Ignatius' Parish status which greatly reduced the church's income. The new brick church became a college church to minister to students, but the Jesuits could not perform weddings or baptisms, prime sources of parish income. The major liturgical services revolved around an academic calendar -- the annual Mass of the Holy Spirit to begin the school year, the All Souls Requiem Mass for deceased students and faculty on November 2nd, and the Baccalaureate Masses for graduation.

St. Ignatius would remain "unparished" until 1994, even though the pre- and post 1906 St. Ignatius churches would be the largest churches in the City.

While the 1868 earthquake did minor damage to St. Ignatius Church, a far more major earthquake was the passage in Sacramento of a new tax law to assess church properties. The church and the college now occupied prime lots on Market Street, so while their church and schools continued to thrive, the taxes took a major financial toll. The debts continued to climb since the costs could not be assessed to working class parents and scholarship students.

By 1878 worshippers spilled into the aisles at hourly Sunday Masses. Enrollments topped 700. It was clear that the Jesuits had outgrown the Market Street "sand dune" property. However, the biggest reason for the move was that enormous property tax bill. The debt now approached $862,510 with a yearly interest alone of $42,500. What did the Jesuits decide to do? Take on more debt and rebuild with a great vision. With Father Maraschi still on hand to raise funds, they envisioned a 2200 seat basilica more fitting for New York, Chicago, or Rome, as well as the largest college campus west of the Mississippi.

During its first 25 years, St. Ignatius Academy had acquired a national reputation and required expanded facilities. SI was especially famous for innovative scientific research in electricity by Father Joseph Neri. He created the first carbon arc spotlights and installed three in the church tower as searchlights to illuminate the Church at night, a dramatic climax for the San Francisco Centennial at the Mechanics Institute. He was also one of the inventors of neon lighting.

Ironically, a hundred years later, PGE would approach the Jesuits with a proposal to illuminate landmarks, starting with the one built on one of the highest hills in the city -- St. Ignatius Church. This pilot project inspired the illumination of the Ferry Building, City Hall, and the War Memorial Opera House, City Hall, and the entire Civic Center.

THE NEW VAN NESS & HAYES CHURCH
AND COLLEGE CAMPUS 1880

FEBRUARY 1, 1880
THIRD ST IGNATIUS – THE BASILICA
FITTING FOR A JESUIT COLLEGE

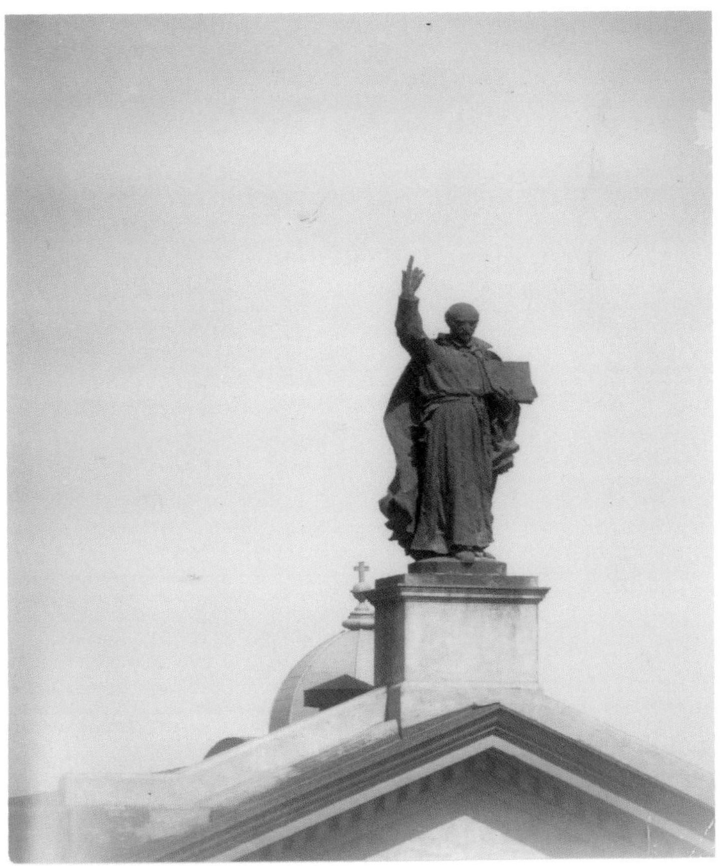

Father General in Rome approved a plan for a new church and campus on less taxable land. It was hoped the sale of the Market Street property, now at the thriving center of the retail district, would cover the debt, the cost of the new land, and the cost of construction. The Jesuits found property further west, again in the sand dunes, again on the outskirts of town. The new lot was a city block-sized parcel in in the Western Addition on Van Ness Avenue between Grove and Hayes, the present-day site of Davies Symphony Hall. The crown jewel of the campus was a 2200 seat "temple worthy of divine worship," the largest basilica west of Chicago at the time. The archbishop celebrated the dedication on Sunday, February 1, 1880.

H. McKeadney, Architect. Houseworth, Photo. 12 Montgomery St. S. F.

SAINT IGNATIUS CHURCH AND COLLEGE,
Cor. Van Ness Avenue and Hayes St. San Francisco, 1878.

The European Baroque church very much mirrored the Gesu Church, the mother church for the Jesuits in Rome. The church entrance was not on Van Ness but on Hayes Street flanked on both sides by the classroom buildings and a Jesuit residence that connected directly to the church. The distinguishing mark for the Hayes Valley location were the twin towers, one of which held Father Maraschi's "firemen's bell" to call congregants to services. The nave of the church was defined by 10 arches in classical Baroque style of the 18th century based on the Roman basilica, or law court, adopted by many early Italian churches. The side areas held many devotional shrines and side altars, again typical of the Baroque style. Debts soon rose to over $1 million dollars before construction was completed. The Jesuits had to abandon plans for decorations appropriate to its architectural style – at least for the time being.

Shortly after the new church was dedicated, the archbishop granted permission for one of San Francisco's largest weddings – the Donohoe/Parrott wedding in 1882. The Donohoe and Parrott families were San Francisco pioneers dating back to 1849, and both families represented two of the city's most powerful banks – Joseph Donohoe the Bank of California, John Parrott of another San Francisco Bank. The newspapers devoted four full page columns to describe the wedding in which the overflowing crowd filled "the whole nave of the church, taxed to its utmost to accommodate the invited guests, whilst the galleries absolutely creaked under a mass of interested humanity." The archbishop himself officiated the wedding service.

The wedding paid off for the Jesuits when sale of the Market Street property stalled during a national economic downturn. Mrs. Parrott purchased the Market Street property for $900,000 which she considered more a donation to the Jesuits than a financial investment. As a gamble, the Parrott corporation decided the site might serve as a shopping center and built The Emporium, then the city's largest department store. The site still serves as a shopping magnet, present day home to the San Francisco Center, Bloomingdale's, and Nordstrom's.

The second wedding, also celebrated in 1882, was between Frank Sullivan and Alice Phelan. This wedding would also play a major role in St. Ignatius' future on the hilltop with the donation of funds to construct the high school building on Stanyan Street by Senator James Phelan.

STAINED GLASS WINDOWS IN THE HAYES STREET CHURCH 1880-1906

In 1885 when Archbishop Patrick Riordan succeeded Alemany, he offered to restore parish status to St. Ignatius. Father John McGloin in his history of the *Jesuits by the Golden Gate (1969)* explains that

Father Superior General Anderledy in Rome wrote back that it "was his desire to have the Jesuit churches as much as possible free from the burden of parish duties," so he declined the offer.

The church and the college continued to play an influential role in the city. In 1901, when President McKinley visited San Francisco, the entire campus celebrated the presidential visit with bunting and flags adorning the windows on Van Ness Avenue. Students lined the staircases and the balconies to greet him, so the president ordered his carriage stopped in front of the school so he could salute the student body of the largest university in the West.

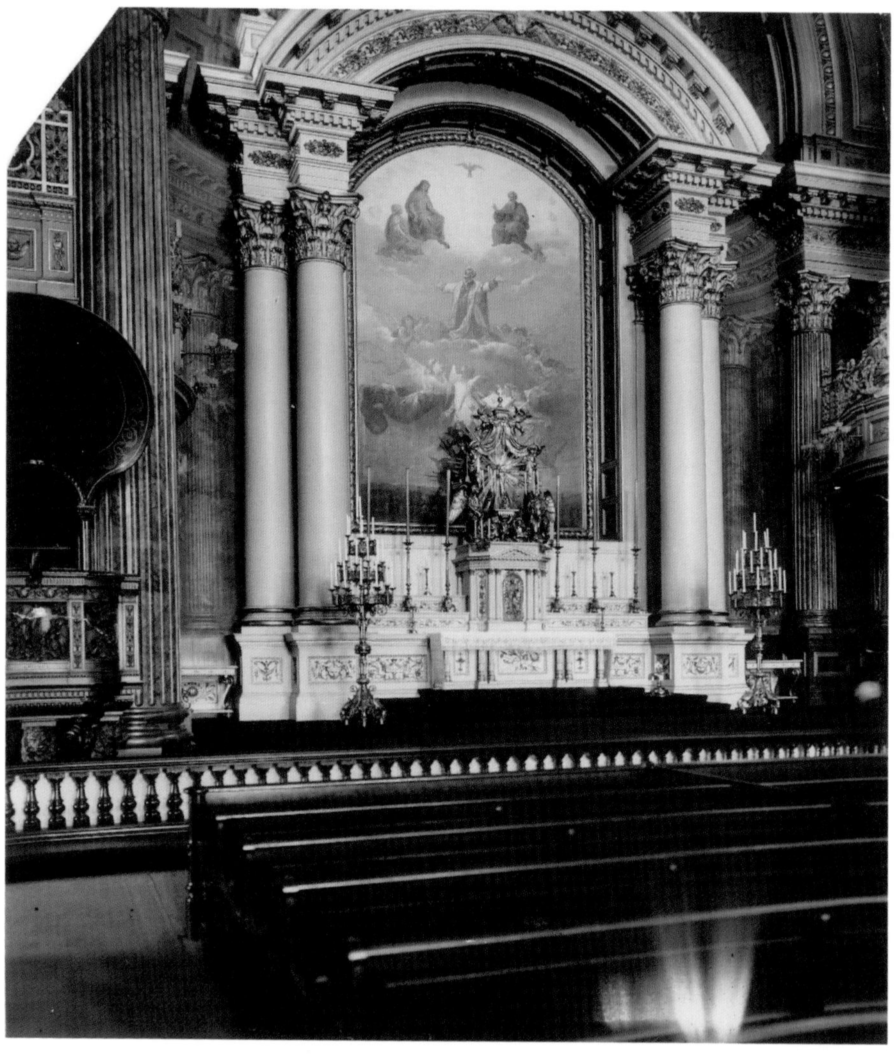

ONE OF THE SIDE ALTAR SHRINES THAT WAS COMPLETED IN TIME FOR THE GOLDEN ANNIVERSARY IN 1905.

Since debts were under $100,000, the Jesuits decided they could finally decorate the new church to celebrate the Jesuit 50th anniversary in San Francisco. By 1890, the interior was finally painted, columns marbleized, medallions and stained-glass windows installed.

In 1895, Bertha Welch (a major benefactress in the years to come) supplied funds for a new organ. Finally, just in time for the Golden Anniversary in 1905, a new tabernacle, main altar, and crown moldings made their appearance. After 50 years of financial struggle, St. Ignatius Church and College – finally free of all debt -- was ready to enter a golden age, sadly a short lived one.

DECORATIONS FOR CHRISTMAS, EASTER AND SPECIAL FEASTS DREW CROWDS TO THE CHURCH. ABOVE ARE DECORATIONS FOR CHRISTMAS MASS 1904.

ST. IGNATIUS CHURCH DECORATIONS FOR THE MEMORIAL MASS FOR POPE LEO XIII IN 1903.

ST. IGNATIUS CHURCH HAS LONG HAD A TRADITION OF ELABORATE CHRISTMAS DECORATIONS. CHRISTMAS MASS 1904.

A SPECIAL JESUIT FEAST IS OUR LADY, THE IMMACULATE CONCEPTION. IN THIS PICTURE ONE NOT ONLY SEES THE ELABORATE DECORATIONS OF THE ENTIRE INTERIOR, BUT ALSO THE SANCTUARY SOCIETY IN FULL REGALIA AND THE WELL-DRESSED CONGREGATION.

Chapter Two

THE EARTH SHOOK, THE SKY BURNED, IGNATIUS IS NO MORE

THE BELL FATHER MARASCHI PURCHASED HAS TRAVELLED TO EACH ST. IGNATIUS CHURCH. EVEN THOUGH THE CHURCH BURNED IN 1906, THE BELL SURVIVED.

At 5:12 am Wednesday, April 18, the San Andreas fault ruptured across 296 miles of California. People as far as Nevada, Los Angeles and Oregon felt the earth move for 48 seconds, an eternity to anyone who has experienced a major quake. The magnitude of the quake has been estimated at close to 8 points on the Richter scale. The extent of the damage was felt throughout Northern California cities. In Santa Rosa over 1000 died, 10% of the town's population. San Jose experienced similar loss of life and property, especially to several local hospitals. Stanford University sustained major damage, especially the collapse of the roof on Memorial Chapel. The estimate of the damages – in 1906 dollars – was over $400,000,000 (today's equivalent of $110 trillion). In a city population of just over 400,000, over half -- 225,000 -- were homeless living in tents in the Presidio and Golden Gate Park.

Surprisingly, St. Ignatius Church sustained minor damage – some candelabra and statues toppled, some plaster fell, but there were no injuries to the Jesuit community. In fact, after a short clean up, the 5:30 morning Mass proceeded as usual. The other morning masses experienced growing congregations with confessional lines stretching down the aisles as aftershocks continued that morning. Many Jesuits left the campus to serve the city population, especially the emergency hospital at the Mechanics Institute. As fires broke out in the downtown areas of the city, St. Ignatius seemed safely removed from the destruction.

A woman who lived at 395 Hayes Street (now site of Caffe Della Steele restaurant) decided to cook breakfast to comfort her family. Since she perceived no major damage to her home, she ignited her stove unaware of the damage to the chimney. Thus, her ham and egg breakfast became the infamous "Ham and Eggs Fire" that consumed the Central Part of San Francisco. The fire was only 3 city blocks from the Church and college, but the winds quickly shifted the flames to the campus.

Father Whittle, the superior of the Jesuit community, wrote in his diary that "What had taken a half century to build up, to equip, now lay in ashes. ... Fire broke out on the westerly tower of our church, and this we extinguished. Then fire broke out on the Easterly tower of our church; this, too, was extinguished; later it broke out in the same tower in a spot which could not be reached without hose and water neither of which could be obtained; at the same time, the easterly tower and the bell tower took fire. The firemen in the tower and our own people then concluded that it was impossible to stop the fire and gave their attention to carrying out the sacred vestments from the church."

CROWDS SADLY WATCH ST. IGNATIUS CHURCH AND COLLEGE BURN IN THE HAM AND EGGS FIRE

The priests in the community managed to save three wagon loads of church art and supplies, but paintings, statues of Carrara marble, a library of 60,000 volumes, and all the Jesuits' personal effects went up in flames. They did, however, manage to save the school and church records by digging a pit, burying the records, and then covering the pit to protect these items from the flames. Weeks later, they returned to retrieve the materials, and all the school records were intact.

The Jesuit community moved into the Holy Family convent atop Fillmore Hill and watched as three major fires in the city joined in one solid holocaust. Jack London, famous California author, visited the city later that day and claimed San Francisco's "surrender was complete ... San Francisco is no more."

Fortunately, his words never reached the Jesuits that night. They were already making plans to rebuild.

PLAN TO REBUILD & PERMISSION FROM THE ARCHBISHOP

On May 7, 1906, two weeks after the earthquake and fire, the Jesuits petitioned Archbishop Riordan and received permission to build a new church and college. The Jesuit community was inspired to aspire: to build a new St. Ignatius worthy of its predecessor. Realtor John Pope, an SI graduate, and architect Joseph Devlin drew up plans for a steel structure to hold 2,000 which they described as "a new temple of worship worthy of God," to establish a new congregation, to create a new San Francisco.

In the meantime, they would build a temporary church on property leased from the Sisters of Mercy across the street from St. Mary's Hospital. On September 15, 1906, the fourth St. Ignatius Church – actually a combination church and college hall – opened. Once again, the Jesuits built on sand dunes on the western outskirts of town. On December 23, 1906, the archbishop dedicated the 500-seat temporary church and temporary college buildings. The temporary wooden structure, which had a maze of stairways and hallways to accommodate for the grade of the lot, did not resemble the hallowed halls of higher education, but more a sweat shop factory somewhere south of Market – hence, the nick name "The Shirt Factory."

Paul Totah in *Spiritus Magis*, notes that by the end of 1907 the Jesuits "determined that they had distributed communion 68,000 times that year." The Jesuit mission, while in temporary quarters, did not diminish. Everyone – especially alumni – dreamed of a new church to replace the splendors of the basilica on Van Ness, but not everyone dreamed of the same location for the new church.

THE 4TH ST. IGNATIUS CHURCH INTERIOR
– THE SHIRT FACTORY CHURCH

1906 – 1910
CASTING LOTS WITH LOTS TO THINK ABOUT

Once the "temporary" church and school opened, the Jesuits entered a four-year discernment process about where to rebuild. Most of the Italian Jesuits in the community wanted to rebuild on Van Ness Avenue since it would be the center of the new city – which turned out to true since it was kitty corner from the future City Hall. The American members of the community, led by the college president

Father John Frieden, opposed rebuilding on Van Ness because of the increasing property taxes and commercialization of the neighborhood. Father Friedan began exploring the neighborhood around the Shirt Factory, and he devised what would become a controversial plan of action.

Father Friedan's plan involved selling the Van Ness property and relocating to a lot bounded by Grove, Cole, Shrader and Fulton streets, present site of the Kendrick Law School and across the street from St. Mary's Hospital. Father proposed excavating the hillside in order to build the new church and college. Friedan engaged engineer John Pope, as advisor to the Jesuits. Pope explained the massive expenses and difficulties of building on that site and proposed building on an available lot on the hilltop at Fulton and Parker, adjacent to the Masonic Cemetery. He believed the hilltop location would make St. Ignatius Church a "beacon on the hill" for the entire city from that lot.

THE SHIRT FACTORY CHURCH AND CAMPUS ONCE AGAIN SURROUNDED BY SAND DUNES

John Pope, in a letter to the alumni, argued against the enormous expenses and difficulties of excavating the Hayes lot – grading and bulkheads alone would cost over $40,000, with a large retaining wall the length of the lot, as well as foundations of great depth to protect the structure from future earthquakes. With the cost of the lot at $102,659, he and others believed more money would go into grading the lot than building the structure itself. He noted the Fulton Street lot required no excavation and no retaining wall because the church foundation would rest on bedrock. Further, the Masonic Cemetery Association was in the process of moving all the graves to Colma (by City ordinance), so the site would offer semi-graded land right on the main boulevard that served as the northern boundary for Golden Gate Park --Fulton Street.

Pope argued that the Fulton and Parker location would allow for an "imposing and noble structure" that could be seen from all over the city, "commanding as it does a magnificent view of the surrounding city, hills, bay and ocean." The church would be a landmark that would be "the pride and boast of the people of San Francisco with its towering outlines in views from all parts of the city."

The Jesuit community was divided, like Gaul, into three parts – some wanted to rebuild on Van Ness, some agreed with Father Friedan's Shrader Street hillside site, and some with Pope, Devlin, and most alums for a hilltop church. The regional superior Father George De La Motte wisely resorted to an old fashioned Ignatian "pro-con" written discernment by the members of the Jesuit community. He asked 20 Jesuits to pray and then write their candid opinions about the benefits and deficits of three plans of action which some called "the casting of the lots" on Van Ness, Hayes, or Fulton.

When Father Friedan was reassigned, the final discernment rested in the hands of the new superior, Father Joseph Sasia. He had originally supported the Friedan plan, but was convinced by the outpouring of support in favor of the Fulton location from the alumni. Between March and December of 1909, he approved the purchase of several hilltop parcels of land from the Masonic Cemetery Association and gave his blessing to the John Pope's architectural design. Charles Devlin, the eventual architect, wisely campaigned for a steel structure to withstand any further earthquakes. The basilica would have 10 side altars, 10 confessional stations, 20 Corinthian pillars supporting 20 Ionian pillars, two spires, and a campanile for Father Maraschi's "fireman's bell" that was retrieved from the rubble. The new church would seat 2000. Three noted assistants on the four-year project were structural consultant W.W. Breite, mechanical engineer William E. Leloand, and electoral contractor Charles T. Phillips.

Just as Father Maraschi had great instincts for real estate in both 1855 and 1878, so did the Jesuits that followed him. With the development of the outer sand dunes of the Richmond and Sunset districts, the Western Addition Hilltop location would eventually become the geographical center of the City, and the new St. Ignatius Church would dominate the skyline from all over the City – St. Ignatius was indeed a beacon on the hill for all the city to see.

Chapter Three

ST IGNATIUS & SAN FRANCISCO RISE FROM THE ASHES

1910-1912
GROUND-BREAKING & CORNERSTONE PLACED

The western hilltop overlooking San Francisco Bay, the Golden Gate, and the Pacific Ocean eventually became known as Ignatian

Heights. Father Sasia, the Jesuits, John Pope and many prominent alumni and citizens gathered on the hilltop and broke ground for construction on December 8, 1910, the Feast of the Immaculate Conception, 60 years to the day when Fathers Accolti and Nobli first arrived in San Francisco. They placed the cornerstone from the 1880 church in the foundation for the campanile. (For the church's centennial in 2014, a time capsule containing a century of pictures and documents was added to this site).

The cornerstone from the 1880 church was not the only remnant to make it to the hilltop. Maraschi's bell was planned for the campanile and still calls worshippers in the surrounding area to services. With the original gold-thread vestments, rescued chalices, and several golden candelabra from the Van Ness church, the present church has "relics" of each St. Ignatius Church in San Francisco.

The foundations and steel substructure took only a year to erect, so that on March 24, 1912 the church's own cornerstone could be laid

on Parker Avenue. Archbishop Patrick Riordan and the new Jesuit superior Father Albert Trivelli led a large procession of 5,000 from the "Shirt Factory" up the hill. As Alan Ziajka describes in *Legacy and Promise*, "The ceremony began with a procession from the temporary church on the corner of Hayes and Shrader and headed up two steep blocks to the new church site." In addition to students from the "Shirt Factory" campus, "a detachment of police, followed by a full regimental band … and members of the Men's and Ladies' Sodality of St. Ignatius, and Archbishop Riordan…"

Father Sasia, a noted preacher of very eloquent, but very long sermons, preached that day, but he was unusually brief because an enormous gust of ocean wind scattered his homily manuscript all over the new property. This, of course, did not presage a tradition of short homilies in the years to come, but it did foreshadow the tradition of great preaching "on the hilltop."

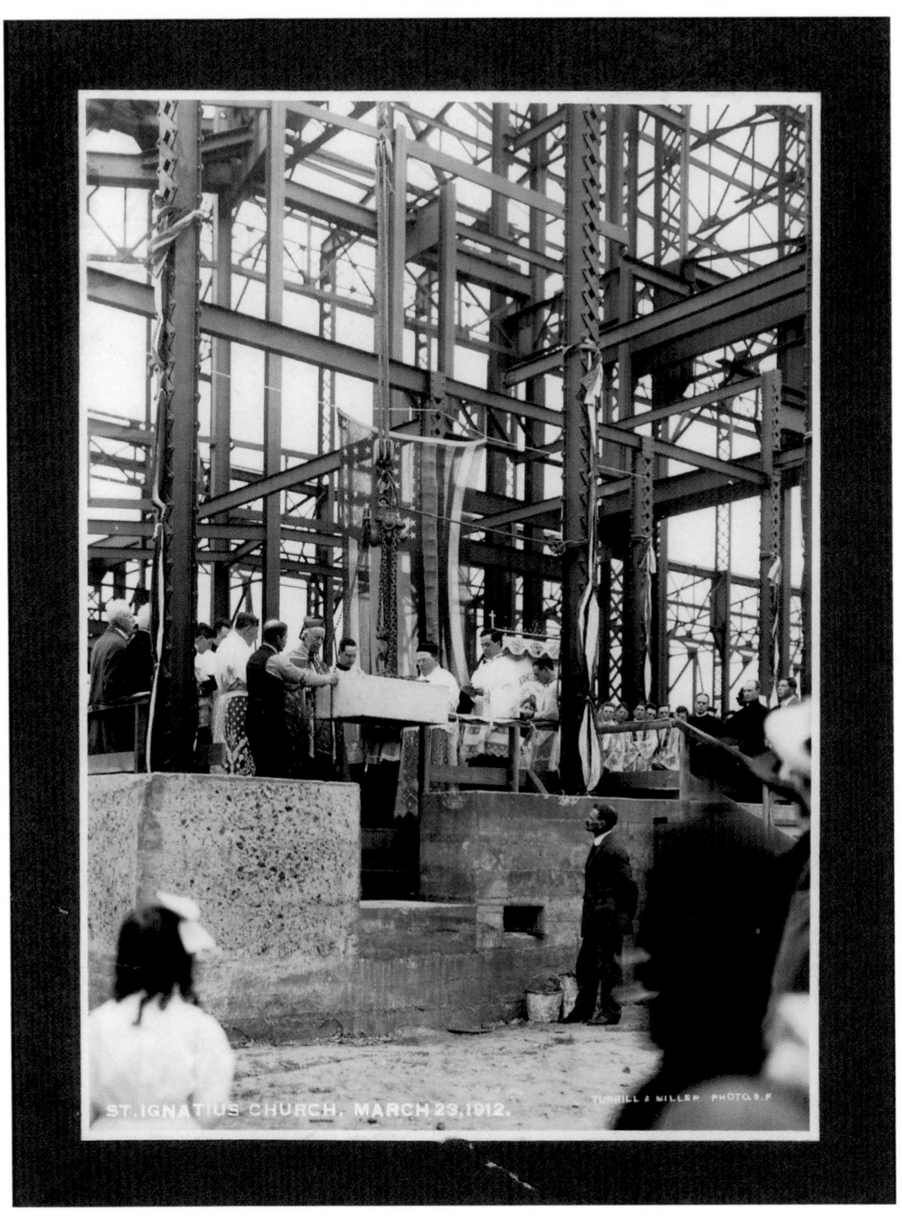

Once the cornerstone was blessed and lowered into place, Father Trivelli read a cablegram from Pope Pius X: "The Holy Father has learned with great pleasure of the laying of the cornerstone of St.

Ignatius Church. He sends best wishes for its completion and imparts on this solemn occasion a special and large apostolic blessing."

The *San Francisco Call* noted that the new building "will be one of the most imposing structures of its kind in San Francisco. Two towers, 230 feet high, will adjoin the nave, which will be 72 feet high, the building covering an area of 271 by 158 feet. The style of the architecture will be Italian Renaissance." The *San Francisco Star* added, "San Franciscans have reason to be proud of the Jesuit Fathers; and with pride, too, they may point to the beautiful temple of worship which soon will crown the heights toward the western sea..." The spires would make St. Ignatius the tallest landmark in the new city skyline – as always, the Jesuits aimed high – and that was true of the new debt.

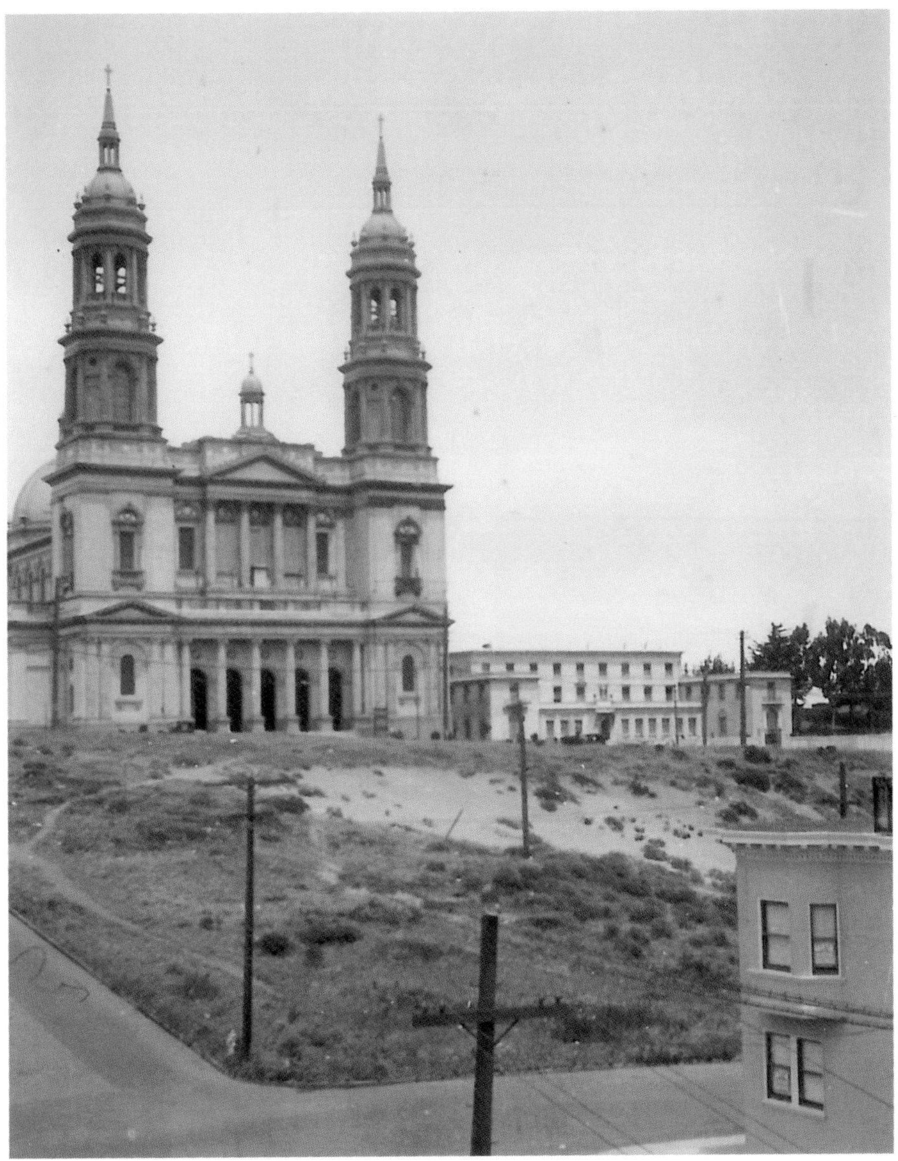

CHAS. J. I. DEVLIN
ARCHITECT
737 PACIFIC BUILDING
HOURS 9 TO 5 P. M.

SAN FRANCISCO, CAL., July 26th, 1912.

Rev. A. F. Trivelli, S.J.
St. Ignatius College.
2211 Hayes Street, City.

Dear Father Trivelli,

In compliance with your verbal request for a statement of the amounts of all contracts awarded to date for the new St. Ignatius Church building, I submit the following:-

To A. Paulsen.------------------------------	Foundation Borings	$ 190.00
" Santa Cruz Portland Cement Co.---------	Cement	7234.50
" " " " "	"	14.70
" John B. Leonard.------------------------	Consulting Engineer	250.00
" Stanquist and Forbes------------------	Concrete	22665.33
" " " " ----------------	"	6570.00
" Central Iron Works--------------------	Steel	82021.50
"O'Connor and Collins--------------------	Masonry	85036.00
"John J. Hughes-------------------------	Carpentry	88235.00
" The J. Looney Co.----------------------	Plumbing	6859.00
" Continental Fireproofing Co.----------	Fireproofing	7000.00
" Forderer Cornice Works----------------	Sheet Metal	38700.00
" Musto-Keenan Co. ---------------------	Marble	4740.00
" Mangrum and Otter----------------------	Heating & Ventilating	8435.00

" Robert W. Hunt and Co.(Inspection.)-----Contract not complete. It is based on unit price per ton for steel, and per barrel for cement.

" Santa Cruz Portland Cement Co.---Contract not complete. It is based on unit price per barrel of ce-

Over 357 $ 49

The cost of construction was estimated to be close to $500,000 –an enormous sum for that era, but more enormous when calculated in

2018 dollars at over $13 million. The Jesuits would once again go into major debt in order to secure the land and commence construction, but hoped the eventual sale of the Van Ness property would cover the costs. In the meantime, the Jesuit community decided they would do without a residence and would sleep in the classrooms so the church could be completed. They did for 7 years until Bertha Welch donated Welch Hall on the lawn adjacent to the church.

CONSTRUCTION AND DESIGN

Construction utilized 100 tons of steel clad with more than 250,0000 bricks and 4000 barrels of cement. The exterior is 154 feet on Fulton Street, 263 feet on Parker Street, and the East and West towers rise to 213 feet. The bell tower (campanile) is 18 foot square and rises to 150 feet. The interior would comprise the largest church west of the Mississippi at that time: The Nave 60 feet by 150 feet, the sanctuary 60 by 62 feet, and a 50 feet diameter dome that rises 150 above the foundations. From the church floor to the heavily decorated ceiling is 74 feet.

Charles Devlin's overall vision was a European Baroque Basilica of the Italian Renaissance, but the front facade with the superimposed colonnades framed by tall towers is more reminiscent of Sir Christopher Wren's St. Paul's Cathedral in London (1657). The details of the exterior and the restrained ornamentation are also in keeping with English examples, but the overall proportions and composition have a marked vertical emphasis more typical of Italian or Spanish Baroque. A notable feature of the exterior is the rhythmic use of massive columns and pilasters of the Ionic and Corinthian Orders. The Ionic is easily recognized by the spiral scrolls on either side of the capitals, like a ram's horns; the Corinthian bears a capital enriched by carved acanthus leaves. The Orders appear as pillars – flat strips on the plane – wrapping the corners and base on the towers, as if the columns were half-embedded in the walls on Parker Street. The campus side has less ornamentation because the original intention was to build a Jesuit residence that would connect to the church.

THE UNDECORATED, UNPAINTED
INTERIOR FROM 1914 UNTIL 1964

The most unusual feature of the columns both inside and outside the church is their bowed shape. The ancient Greeks learned that tapering the column shafts toward the top created a better proportion and appearance, but St. Ignatius incorporates tapering at both the top and the bottom of the columns, what architects call a *double entasis.*

THE UNDECORATED, UNPAINTED
INTERIOR FROM 1914 UNTIL 1964

The new church incorporated many of the features of the Van Ness church destroyed in 1906, especially the twin towers and the classical Corinthian columns. The nave of the church is defined by 20 columns with Corinthian tops that created nine arches that repeat the pattern in the sanctuary in classical Baroque style of the 18th century. The general layout is based on designs of many early churches, such as the first St. Peter's or St. Mary Major in Rome -- a wide nave to allow the congregation to easily hear and see the preacher and presider.

The semi-circular sanctuary is 60 x 62 feet, fronted by marble stairs. Above the main altar is a convex dome – 50 feet in diameter – covered by an exterior dome directly above, a separate structure that rises 152 feet from the ground clad in sheet metal, as is the main roof of the church. A stained-glass window caps the dome and depicts the Holy Spirit watching over the entire church and congregation. In the sanctuary are semicircular arches on columns with Corinthian capitals creating a gallery, or ambulatory (translation -- "you can still see"). This is a remnant of a planned adjoining Jesuit residence and remained unused for 50 years until 1964 when the organ pipes were moved from the highest gallery to behind the main altar.

The plaster ornamentation incorporates three major imagistic sources: angels, humans, and nature with constructive boxes upholding the human statues, the columns upholding the leaves, and the arches upholding the angels, all reaching up to the heavens.

A CHURCH OF MANY ROOFS

When a person looks at the roof from the outside, the church appears to have one solid roof and a rounded dome not unlike St. Peter's in Rome. It is one of the greater illusions designed into the exterior church structure. St. Ignatius Church does not have just one roof but a series of roofs— a dozen. This complicates the drainage of rain water especially during heavy downpours and adds to the challenges of roof maintenance. In addition, there is a huge amount of sheet metal encasing the steeples, roof ledges and bell tower which needs constant attention. The metal on the dome was covered with sheet metal, necessarily replaced in the late 1990's with lead-coated copper.

Originally a series of interior drainage pipes made of galvanized metal passed through the center of metal columns at the side altars of the church. These galvanized pipes soon deteriorated, and water passed through the walls. Instead of replacing the extremely hard to access pipes, during the 1920s a series of exterior drainage pipes was added. These exterior pipes, as well as the scupper drains (metal lined spaces cut along the borders of the roof for the water to pass through until it reaches the drains), eventually deteriorated. More drainage pipes were added, and the metal scuppers were substantially repaired or replaced in 2003-2004.

The interior dome is not the same as the exterior dome, nor is it a dome within a dome. They are actually two separate domes. Similarly, the side altars all have domes, but these are not the actual roofs of the side chapel structures.

Like the Golden Gate bridge which is always being painted to protect it from rusting in the salt sea air, the multiple roofs of St. Ignatius continuously require repair and maintenance in order to protect the steel structure and the elaborate plasterwork. Usually this results in a campaign to raise $500,000-800,000 every 20-25 years.

AUGUST 2, 1914
DEDICATION OF THE UNPAINTED & UNDECORATED CHURCH

The Fathers of St. Ignatius University

Request the pleasure of your company at the

Dinner

to be given on the occasion of the

Dedication of St. Ignatius Church

August 2nd, 1914

Dinner immediately after the Dedication Services

Please return enclosed card, signifying your acceptance

to

Rev. A. F. Trivelli, S. J.

2211 Hayes St.

The church – the largest West of Chicago -- celebrated its first Mass on August 2, 1914. However, it was unpainted and undecorated since cost overruns dictated there would be no pulpit, no statues, no shrines, no stained-glass windows, no side altars. The church was hardly completed – in fact, the plaster remained unpainted for 48 years, the "temporary wooden altar" from the Shirt Factory lasted for 35 years, and there were no stained-glass windows for another 25 years.

Due to cost overruns, the plans to paint and decorate the church had to be scrapped. Therefore, the only interior decoration was provided by the Stations of the Cross paintings which arrived from Rome October 14, 1914. The Stations of the Cross were formally blessed on All Saints Day, November 1, 1914. Professor Piertro Rudolphi painted fourteen murals measuring five feet by ten feet; each cost the then large sum of $375 each ($10,000 each in today's equivalency). When Father Gagan consulted the family about restoration of these paintings in 1998, the family told him that the members of the Rudolphi family posed for those 14 original paintings.

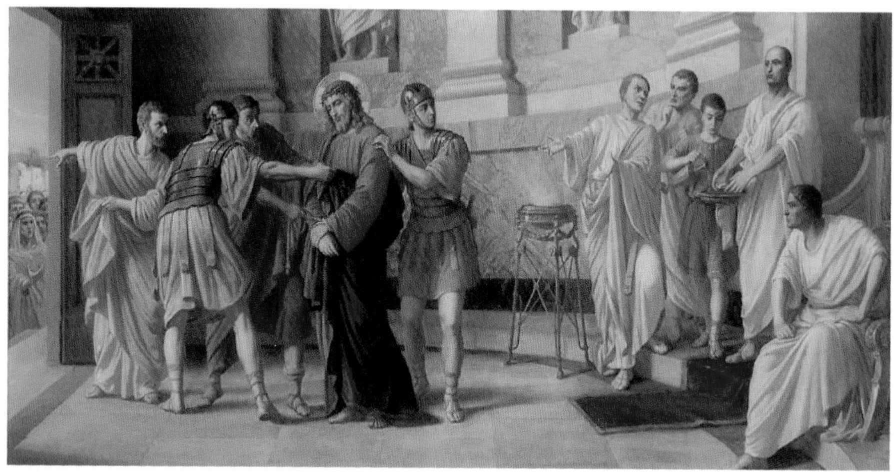

Unfortunately, insurance and property sale on Van Ness did not provide the expected funds, so the Jesuits faced an $800,000 debt (over $23 million in 2018 dollars). Finally, the debt became a major crisis and threatened the future of the Jesuits in San Francisco.

1919-1925
"SAVE ST. IGNATIUS" CHURCH CAMPAIGN

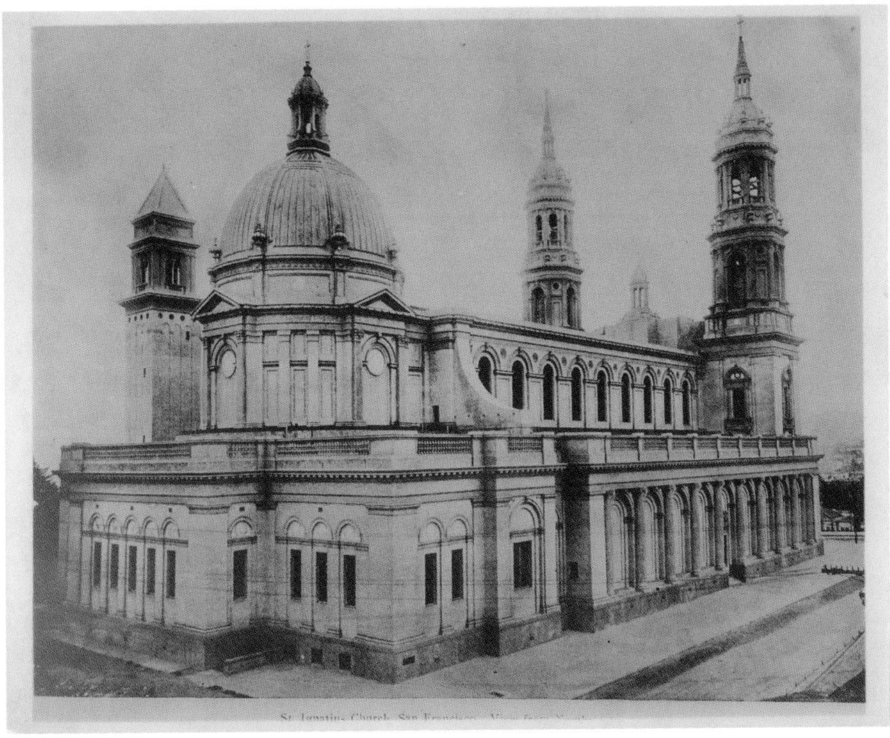

With the United States entry into World War I, the country experienced a serious financial crisis. Enrollments dropped, tuitions went unpaid, and debts mounted. The Jesuits struggled to pay the monthly interest rate, and the banks threatened foreclosure. Father Francis Dillon, provincial of the California Jesuits, met with Archbishop Hanna and several prominent businessmen and alumni. They decided to launch a "Save St. Ignatius" campaign in each and every parish church in the diocese. On April 15, 1919, Archbishop Hanna issued a proclamation calling for the all of the citizens of San Francisco to come to the aid of St. Ignatius: "The Jesuit Fathers of San Francisco have for some time past been struggling under an insupportable burden of debt, which growing heavier from day to day, {of} such alarming proportions that it has moved the friends of St. Ignatius Church and college to make a supreme effort to relive the lamentable condition. Something must be done and quickly..."

San Francisco newspapers joined the campaign urging citizens to support the church and college. The *San Francisco Call*, on June 2, 1919, declared "St. Ignatius is San Francisco itself ... every citizen is a son of the old college ... {we} now ask those sons to keep death away from its doors. They ask one million dollars to give back to St. Ignatius the strength it had before the fire. In withholding aid, San Francisco kills part of itself. In giving this money, it gives life to a force that must never die."

An executive committee formed including the archbishop, the mayor James Rolph, Jr, SI graduate US Senator James Phelan, and prominent business leaders such as William Crocker, Herbert Fleischacker, and Daniel Murphy – Protestant, Jewish and Catholic leaders, one of the first inter-faith ecumenical coalitions in San Francisco history. On May 12 of that year, an alumni banquet was held at the St. Francis Hotel with 400 in attendance where Senator Phelan presented the Jesuits with a check for $10,000 to start the campaign. The world-famous Irish tenor John McCormack provided the entertainment. By 1925, after yearly fundraisers and the generosity of San Franciscans and the special generosity of alumni, the church "with the spires that inspire" was safe from its creditors. The Archbishop celebrated the debt reduction and called the church a symbol for the city which rose from the ashes and demonstrated the human spirit to aspire to new life.

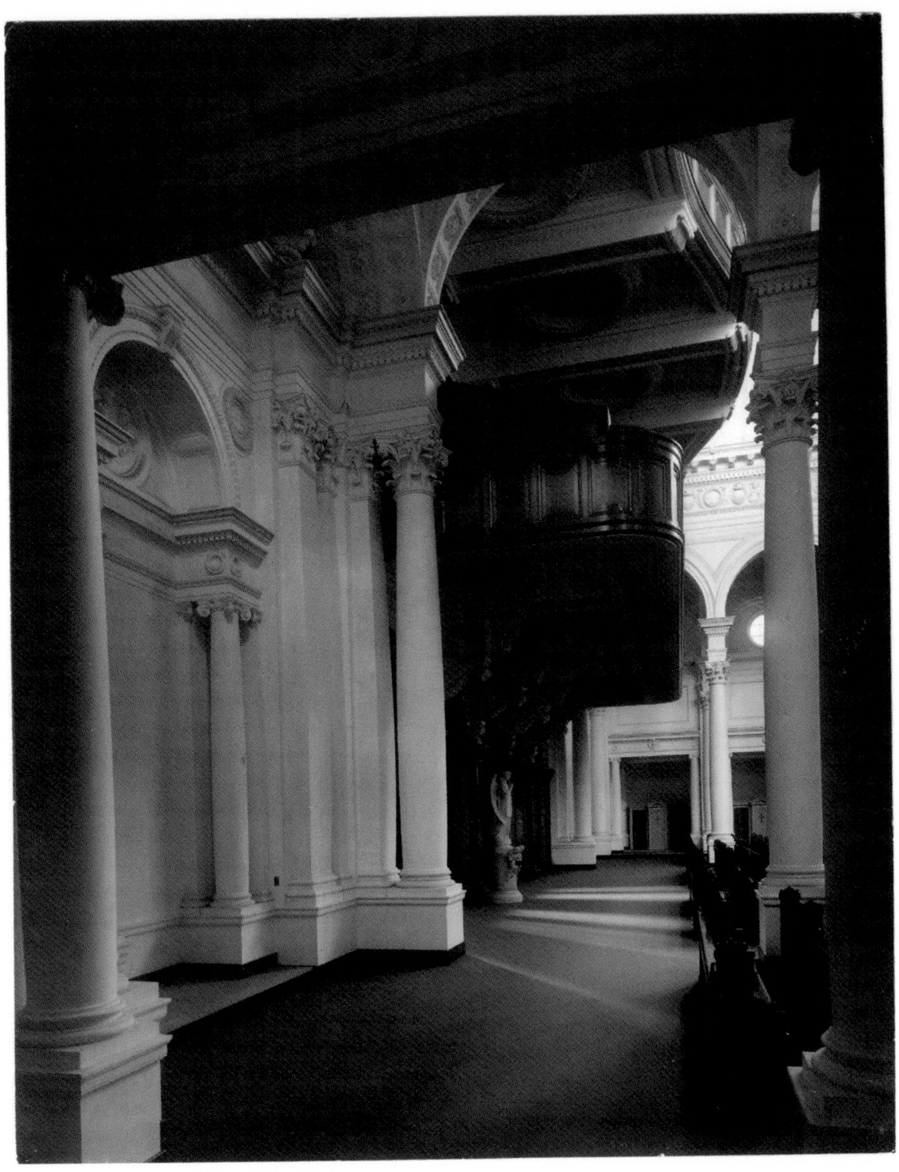

Parts of the church remained undecorated until the late 1950s and early 1960s. This blank alcove is now the shrine of St. Ignatius.

Chapter Four

UNIQUE JESUIT TRADITIONS

MINISTERS AT THE ALTAR

The tradition of involving the laity in ministry dates back to the tradition of acolytes, now known as altar servers. When those three young men enrolled in 1855, they formed the parish's first organization, the Sanctuary Society. Since every Jesuit had to offer Mass daily, there was a great need for altar servers as the size of the Jesuit faculty grew. Of course, the "Sanc Society," as it was nicknamed, provided a great source of vocations. By 1951 over a third of the priests at the university and high school were former sanctuary society members. With the relocation of the high school in 1969, the university folded the sanctuary society into the campus ministry program. In 1994, Father Gagan reformed the sanctuary society as a girls' and boys' organization of active young altar servers. The current parish involves adult and youth parishioners as altar servers, lectors, Eucharistic ministers, and cantors, so the ministry of serving at liturgies has expanded and involves a substantial number of parishioners.

TRADITION OF GREAT JESUIT PREACHERS

From the first great Jesuit preacher James Bouchard at the Market Street Church in 1861, St. Ignatius has always enjoyed a long-standing tradition of scholarly and inspirational preachers. The first of a series of lecture-sermons in the new hilltop church on "Genuine and Pseudo Christian Science" occurred in 1915 by Father Dennis Kavanagh, SJ. His direct, simple style had great appeal, so the church was packed to overflowing. In Lent of 1917 he returned with another series entitled: "War, Civilization, and Christianity" and again 1923 on "Bigotry and Intolerance." His voice projected throughout the church to overflowing crowds without the aid of microphones, even without the aid of the high pulpit with its resounding wooden roof.

During the 1920s and 1930s, St. Ignatius Church offered something unique – a "Doctor's Retreat" – open to all medical professionals Catholic and non-Catholic. Throughout the years, due to USF's Law School, the church also became known as the Lawyer's Church. During the late 1920s and early 1930s the most popular preacher was Father Charles Carroll. Every year the Jesuits would host a Lenten Novena of Grace which would culminate on the feast of the canonization of St Ignatius Loyola and St. Francis Xavier, March 12th. Father John McGloin in *Jesuits By the Golden Gate* estimates that during the 1940s St. Ignatius Church would host 3500 to 4000 for Sunday Masses, a tradition that continued well into the 1970s. Sunday congregations have been held spellbound by Fathers Raymond Feeley, William Dunne, William Richardson, William Ryan, John Coleman, visiting Jesuit scholars and missionaries from all over the Catholic world, and past and current pastors Charles Gagan and Greg Bonfiglio. Since the bulletin frequently announces homilists a week in advance, churchgoers often choose to attend services for a specific homilist.

SPECIAL CELEBRATIONS –JESUIT JUBILEES, ORDINATIONS, CIVIC FUNERALS

THE DIAMOND JUBILEE MASS OUTDOORS ON THE FIELD FOR THE HIGH SCHOOL CAMPUS.

Due to its grand size, St. Ignatius Church has been the scene of many special liturgical celebrations – from Jesuit Ordinations to Jesuit Jubilees to important civic funerals to the annual university and high school celebrations. In Jesuit schools the academic year commences with a Mass of the Holy Spirit and ends with a Baccalaureate Mass.

The church has been the scene of both SI and USF graduations, as well as graduations for other Catholic schools such as Presentation Academy and Mercy Burlingame. Two special Jesuit occasions were the visitations by the General of the Jesuits, by Father Arrupe in the early 1970s, then again by Father Hans Kovenbach in 2007.

THE HOLY THURSDAY ALTAR OF REPOSE FOR THE BLESSED SACRAMENT. THE CHURCH STAYED OPEN ALL NIGHT AS CONGREGANTS KEPT WATCH WITH THE BLRSSED SACRAMENT UNTIL GOOD FRIDAY SERVICES.

The first of larger funeral liturgies was offered for benefactress Bertha Welch who offered her home to the Jesuits after the earthquake and fire, then made major donations for the church building fund and for a Jesuit Residence, which stood adjacent to the church (currently a lawn). Other major funeral celebrations included Alumnus Senator James D. Phelan, also a former mayor, who donated funds for the high school building on Stanyan Street. Throughout World Wars I and II memorial Masses for SI and USF graduates were solemn occasions, as were the ROTC Military Masses on November 2nd, feast of All Souls, up to the late 1960s. Several prominent Jesuits, faculty members, graduates, and lay persons have been buried from St. Ignatius Church throughout the years, from former university presidents Fathers Dunne, Connolly, Dullea and LoSchiavo to prominent judges and attorneys, to members of the SF Police and Fire Departments.

THE MILITARY MASSES

During both World Wars, St. Ignatius Church celebrated special liturgies to commemorate the graduates of the high school and college serving in the military. Starting in 1942, USF became one of the most active ROTC campuses in the area, so barracks soon appeared on campus, and the annual ROTC Military Mass was celebrated every Veterans Day. The sanctuary featured a service flag with silver and gold stars for injured and deceased military graduates; by 1944 the flag was adorned with over 300 stars.

The parish continued this tradition during the Korean Conflict and the Vietnam War. Every year on Veteran's Day, the university celebrated the annual Military Mass. ROTC cadets would march the colors down the main aisle, and at the consecration the cadets would form an arch with their swords to honor the Blessed Sacrament, then at the end of Mass the "Star Spangled Banner" would be played on trumpet followed by the recessional.

During the Vietnam conflict ROTC was still mandatory for all male students during their first two years of enrollment. Because of the unpopularity of the war, many students began protesting not only the war, but the program's presence on campus. Faculty and students often debated the merits of the just war theory on an almost daily basis in the Harney Plaza at lunch times. Eventually, students staged a respectful silent protest at the Veteran's Day Military Mass. In 1969 the university ceased requiring ROTC, and by 1970 the long-standing tradition of the Military Mass was discontinued. The banners with the gold and silver stars are still carefully maintained in the parish archives.

MILITARY ROTC MASS DURING WWII

Jesuit Jubilees – St. Ignatius has been fortunate to celebrate many priesthood jubilees, the most recent for Father John Coleman on the 50th anniversary of his ordination in St. Ignatius Church. One of the most famous was the 60th Jubilee for Father Richard Gleeson. The celebration involved not only the high school, university and alumni, but the mayor of San Francisco Angelo Rossi and brother of Bank of America founder A.P. Giannini -- Doctor A. H. Giannini. The Diamond Jubilee in 1955 reached its climax when Jesuits from all over the West joined representatives from every major religious order, the pastors of the diocesan parishes, and Archbishop John M. Mitty. In recent years, the jubilee celebrations of Jesuits 50 years of priesthood have included such popular preachers as Fathers John Coleman, Charles Gagan, and John LoSchiavo.

"Tre Ore" on Good Friday – As part of the third week of Ignatius Loyola's Spiritual Exercises, Ignatius asks the retreatant to imagine being in Jerusalem when Jesus is condemned to die, then to accompany Jesus on the Way of the Cross, and to be with Jesus at the crucifixion. This eventually led a particular Jesuit tradition of Three Hours on Good Friday. One Jesuit would take on the task of guiding the congregation through the Passion of Christ, sometimes focusing on the Stations of the cross, sometimes on the Seven Last Words, sometimes on being present with Mary. These powerful meditations became enormously popular, and in San Francisco eventually led to the Reverent Observance of Good Friday when most stores, theatres, and businesses would close down from 12 – 3pm. Many parish churches adopted the tradition, but St. Ignatius has always been a magnet for packed congregations during the Three Hours. Father John Coleman has been especially dedicated to continuing this tradition at St. Ignatius – it is the oldest tradition dating back to 1856.

THE UNDECORATED CHURCH WITH THE CHANDELIER OVER THE ALTAR RAIL CIRCA 1955

"Te Deum" on New Year's Eve: Another long-standing Jesuit tradition throughout the world is to sing the "Te Deum" hymn on New Year's Eve. This early hymn of praise – sometimes called the Ambrosian Hymn or Song of the Church – is part of the daily office, but the Jesuits instituted a special New Year's Eve liturgical service that involved the sacrament of confession and the singing of the "Te Deum" to thank God for the blessings of the old year and ask God's blessings for the New Year. The uniquely Jesuit aspect is that this is the hymn Edmund Campion and the English Jesuit martyrs sang after they were sentenced to death in Elizabethan England. The final "Te Deum" service was held on New Year's Eve 1970 for a small, faithful congregation of alumni, including this author's father who had attended since 1920.

RELICQUARY

Among the holy relics possessed by St. Ignatius Church are several relics of the True Cross and also a reliquary dating from the 1920's which has several dozen relics of the Jesuit saints who had been beatified and canonized up to that time. These relics are often brought out for veneration on the feast of Jesuit saints, on Good Friday and the feast of the Holy Cross. One of the relics of the True Cross possessed by the church of the True Cross was given to the church by the Religious of the Sacred Heart in the 1990's. Along with the relic is stored a letter dating from 1915 written by Archbishop Riordan to the mother superior of the Religious of the Sacred Heart stating that the relic had been given by Pope Pius IX to Dennis J. Oliver, a great benefactor of the Jesuits and the Catholic Church in San Francisco starting in the 1850's. Mr. Oliver had given a silver brick to Pope

Pius IX from which the Pope struck medals for the bishops in attendance at Vatican Council I which ended in 1870. Mr. Oliver gave the relic to Archbishop Riordan who gave it to the Religious of the Sacred Heart around 1900, then the Religious of the Sacred Heart gave it to Fr. Gagan and St. Ignatius Church in 2000.

THE MEN'S AND LADIES' SODALITIES

A tradition of Jesuit churches has always been not only the evangelization of converts, but the spiritual growth of the faithful. For the Jesuits, this often involved creating small spiritual communities where the congregants could experience the Spiritual Exercises of St. Ignatius. "Sodality" refers to a lay society for religious and charitable purposes. The first Sodality at St. Ignatius, founded in 1859, was only for students, but adult groups soon formed. By 1870 the members of "Our Lady's Sodality" had grown to over 120 students, a full quarter of the student body. When the organization was open to adult men, especially alumni, the Sodality quickly grew to over 400. "The Gentleman's Sodality" became actively involved in special liturgical celebrations, developed a church library of spiritual books, and attended Mass together every Sunday. By 1900 the Sodality had grown to over 1000 members. After the earthquake and fire, both groups held fund-raisers for the new church. By the 1940s, with the advent of other Catholic organizations, membership declined, and the last meetings were held in the 1960s. The current parish has formed men's and women's prayer groups, annual retreats, and hosts social ministries that continue the Sodality tradition.

LOYOLA GUILD

One fundraising group still continues to this day, the Loyola Guild. At the suggestion of several mothers of students, Father Edwin McFadden, SJ helped organize women whose sons attended or had graduated from St. Ignatius, or were wives of professors, or were mothers of Jesuits to "foster a deeper acquaintance with all in touch with St. Ignatius." The first women, led by Mrs. Frank Silva and Mrs. George Devine, held a bake sale and brought the profits to the Jesuit house. Father William Dunne reported years later that those funds answered the Jesuit community's prayers – it paid the long overdue electric bill.

The Guild continued to raise funds for scholarships for both the high school and university, holding annual luncheons, rummage sales, house tours and other fundraisers. The Guild celebrated its 50th anniversary in the Gold Ballroom of the Palace Hotel, and its 75th anniversary in Carlin Commons on the SI campus. Loyola Guild is still active and has raised over half a million dollars in scholarship funds for both the high school and the university.

BERTHA WELCH

The most instrumental lay person in the early development of the current St. Ignatius Church was Bertha Welch (1849-1922). Born in Paris, she later married a wealthy New Orleans businessman who made a fortune in sugar. The family settled in San Francisco in the 1880s, and her three sons attended St. Ignatius on Van Ness. She made her first donation to Father Aloysius Varsi for art and paintings. Several years later, she donated $50,000 for the largest church organ west of the Mississippi. It was described as "the king of Instruments" according to local newspapers. Her donations continued to help complete the decoration of the church in time for the University's Golden Anniversary in 1905.

In 1906 while visiting New York, Bertha read of the destruction and immediately contacted the Jesuits who temporarily lived at the Holy Family Convent atop Fillmore Street. She made her residence at 1090 Eddy Street near Alamo Square available for the Jesuits. She continued to contribute to the new church building fund, and shortly before her death in 1922 she presented a final gift to her beloved Jesuit fathers – funds for a faculty residence. Her funeral service included Jesuits from throughout the California Province as well as numerous alumni; however, a special feature picked up in the local newspapers was the large San Francisco Chinese delegation for whom she was also a great advocate and philanthropist.

Since she did not specify the amount of funds for the Jesuit community, her relatives decided to cut back on some of the original plans and building materials. Original plans called for joining the residence to the church, but Welch Hall ended up being a free-`standing building next to the church. Eventually the Jesuit community expanded to the point that only the college Fathers lived in the residence; the high school Jesuits lived on rollaway beds and sleeping bags in the military barracks built during the second world war. In 1959, the university applied for a federal grant to build a faculty residence Xavier Hall, so the high school Jesuits occupied the slowly deteriorating structure. When the high school moved to the Sunset in 1969, USF used the building for one semester until it was determined to be unsafe; it was demolished in 1972.

Chapter Five

FIFTY YEARS OF DELAYED DECORATION

Before the Vatican Council in 1962, each priest celebrated daily Mass, so most university churches incorporated numerous side altars for this purpose. St. Ignatius Church has 5 on each side. It was not unusual to hear a cacophony of consecration bells from 9 different altars from 5am until 8am every morning. Since there were also three altars in the sacristy area, one often heard "ghost" bells as well.

Blessed Mother's Altar (and the baptismal font) was blessed and dedicated on the feast of the Assumption, August 15, 1924, the gift of Mr. Owen McHugh in memory of his wife Bridget Fitzpatrick. The statue of Our Lady is of pure Carrara marble. The chapel, donated in memory of Thomas J. Wattson in 1936, was restored in loving memory of Rebecca Diepenbrock DelSanto by Lawrence A. DelSanto and DelSanto children. The special feature of the DelSanto family restoration project was the multiple of 12 – 12 wooden chairs and 12 candles on the altar – one for each of the Del Santo children. Joel

Villanon received national awards for his work on this and several other design projects in the church. .

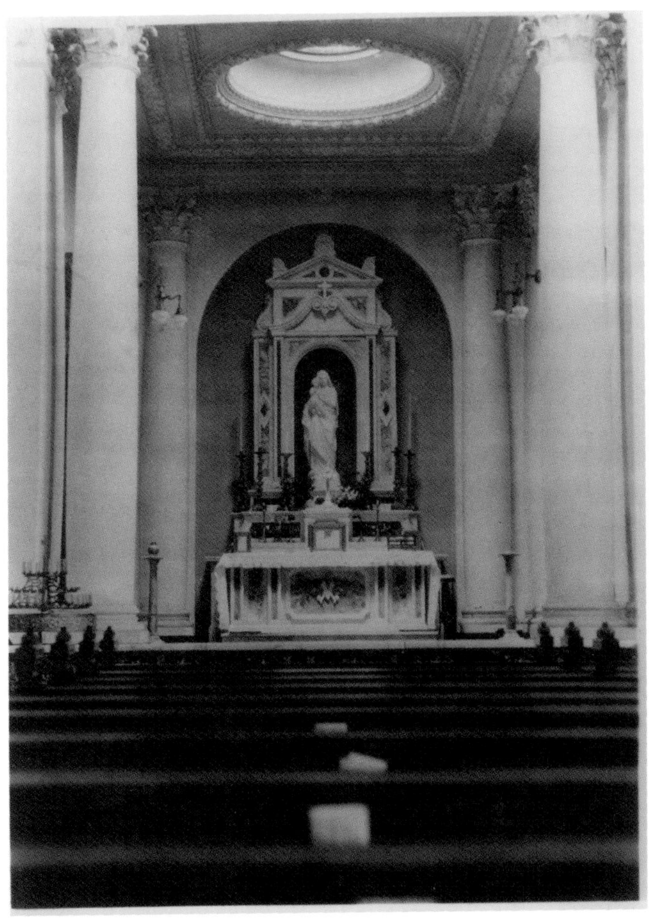

In the ceiling is a stained-glass oculus created by Father Thomas Lucas, SJ. Above the west sacristy door is Antonio Dolfi's year 2000 reproduction of the c. 1475 Andrea della Robbia blue and white glazed terracotta Annunciation. The original, located in the Upper Church at La Verna (Arezzo, Italy), shows Mary seated with a book of prayer and holding her hand in a gesture of reverence; the scene includes the archangel Gabriel, a vase of lilies (symbol of Mary's purity), God the Father, six cherubim and a dove representing the Holy Spirit. The text Mary is reading is from Isaiah: "Behold a virgin will give birth."

There are three other della Robbia art works in the church, two in the Baptismal chapel. One of Mary hangs on the wall of the Calegari-Blaettler inner chapel with the baptismal font, the other of Madonna and Child hangs in the chapel vestibule. The final della Robbia work hangs in the Reconciliation chapel.

St, Joseph's Altar, donated by Mrs. Mary Gartland in memory of her husband Patrick, was blessed and dedicated on October 5, 1924. In 2002 the Katherine Walsh Foundation and Jerry and Geraldine Cole commissioned new flooring, lighting, sound and decoration. St. Joseph's altar, closest to the sacristy, has become the altar for daily Masses and also received awards for its re-design by Joel Villanon.

PARKER AVENUE SIDE ALTARS:

Saint Aloysius Gonzaga (1568-1591) Gonzaga, a Jesuit novice, died at the age of 23 and is the patron saint of young students. The paintings show him receiving his first communion and caring for the sick in Rome. Above the altar is a portrayal of Gonzaga's vision of St. Mary Magdalen. Altar and chapel were completed and blessed in 1927.

The Sacred Heart of Jesus: St. Margaret Mary Alacoque had a vision of the Sacred Heart of Jesus which she shared with Jesuit priest St. Claude de La Columbiere who spread the devotion throughout the world. The right painting portrays Columbiere entering the Society of Jesus. The left painting left shows St. Margaret Mary Alacoque's vision of the Sacred Heart, with another depiction above the altar. Completed and blessed in 1914 by auxiliary Bishop Hanna, the shrine is a donation of the League of the Sacred Heart. This as the first side chapel completed after the church opened.

St. Robert Bellarmine (1542-1621) A teacher and writer, and theologian of the Council of Trent, the painting on the left shows him teaching, while the right shows him as spiritual father to St. Aloysius

Gonzaga. His portrait hangs above the altar. The Bellarmine chapel, gift of Mr. Martin O'Brien in memory of his father, was completed and blessed in 1934.

THE CAMPUS SIDE ALTARS:

St. Alphonsus Rodriguez (1533-1617) A Jesuit brother, Rodriguez entered the Society after the tragic death of his wife and sons. The right painting celebrates his work as spiritual director for St. Peter Claver, missionary to the black slaves in America, and the left painting shows Claver ministering to the slaves at Cartagena. The painting above the altar depicts Alphonsus at prayer with Our Lady of Della Strada by Pietro Rudolfi, artist for the stations of the Cross. The chapel was donated by Mrs. Mary Morrissey in 1927.

St. Francis Xavier (1506-1552): One of the first Jesuit companions, Xavier became the first Jesuit missionary to India and Japan.

The painting on the left shows St. Ignatius in Xavier's study asking, "What does it profit a man to gain the world and lose his immortal soul?" The painting on the right shows Xavier preaching in Portugal before his departure for Asia. The painting above the altar captures the moment of his death in the bay of Canton awaiting permission to enter China. This final side altar was dedicated in March 1936, in memory of Mr. and Mrs. Dennis Begley and their son Joseph.

St. Peter Canisius (1521-1597): This famous writer, confessor and Doctor of the Church founded numerous schools and is credited with keeping Vienna and Prague loyal to Catholicism. The painting on the left portrays Canisius at the Council of Trent speaking to Emperor Ferdinand and Cardinal Truchsess. The painting on the right shows him teaching catechism, and the painting above the altar shows Canisius deep in prayer. Completed and blessed in 1934, the gift of Linda and Augustine Berti in memory of their parents.

The paintings of St. Robert Bellarmine and of St. Peter Canisius are the work of the Irish American artist Joseph O'Sullivan. O'Sullivan was one of the early artists of religious art in California. His son Carroll O'Sullivan became a Jesuit of the California Province and served as Provincial.

A special feature of each of these shrines and side altars is that each has its own dome and central skylight. The restoration process and the historical research for the project was done by Father Tom Lucas who also worked on the restoration of Ignatius' chapel in Rome at the Jesuit headquarters. Each of the domes is decorated in gold leaf, specially commission by Father Lucas in 1998.

THE HIGH PULPIT

In 1928 James Lee decided that the Jesuit preachers deserved a better podium for delivering not only Sunday homilies, but also Reflections on the Spiritual Exercises of Ignatius, called Missions. During the 1920 and 1930s, St. Ignatius hosted enormously popular evening series of lectures and homilies on spiritual topics. The preacher had to project to a congregation of 2000 before the age of electronic amplification. Lee's donation of the new pulpit built of solid hand carved oak allowed for a preacher to speak without amplification and still be heard throughout the church since the wooden "ceiling" of the high pulpit acted as a sounding board.

STAINED-GLASS WINDOWS

The original windows of the church, a golden amber glass, can still be seen in the sacristy and the bookshop windows. While these cast a soft glow on the unpainted plaster, the original design called for stained-glass windows to duplicate the effect of the Van Ness church. The project to transform the amber windows began in 1937 and was not completed until 25 years later when the church was redecorated to celebrate its 50th anniversary in 1964.

In 1937, Harold Wilberton Cumming Studios' stained-glass window designer Willemina Ogterop, the first woman to join the Glasziers and Glass Workers Union of San Francisco, fashioned the first of the stained-glass windows. For the next 24 years she and the Cumming Studio artists designed the remaining stained-glass windows as individual donors came forth to complete the project.

The 18 circular triforium windows were installed between 1938 and 1942. The first circular window is of St. Ives, patron saint of lawyers. This is followed by windows celebrating Jesuit heroes St. Andrew Bobola, SJ, a Slavic martyr, and St. Issac Jogues, a North American martyr. Other windows celebrate great Jesuits including Polish Jesuit St., Stanislaus Kostka, St. John Berchmans, St. Robert Bellarmine, St. Aloysius Gonzaga, St. Francis Xavier, and St. Ignatius Loyola. There are windows that depict non-Jesuit saints such as St. Joseph, St. Francis of Assisi, St. Augustine, St. Thomas Aquinas, and St. Cecilia. The five first balcony circular windows converted to stained-glass in 1953.

The 18 Clerestory Windows (top windows) measure nearly 18 feet high. The first to be installed was Christ the King in 1945, and St. Mary Magdalene signaled the completion in 1962 – a 27-year project. Ironically, the addition of stained-glass windows greatly reduced the natural lighting in the church finally corrected in the interior painting and relighting of the church in 1962.

Names and Sequence of the Stained Glass Windows, Saint Ignatius Church

All of the windows were made by the Cummings Studios in San Francisco, California. Willemina Ogterop led the design and creation process for the windows. She was assisted by Norbert Graves, a former seminarian, in the development of the windows' iconography between 1939 and 1941. The funding for the stained glass windows began in 1937, driven and collected by the Graduate School of Law at USF. The project was directed by A. Russel Berti, an alumni and professor at Hilltop. The first commissioned window was St. Ives - a circular stained glass window with the iconography of St. Ives, patron saint of lawyers. The window cost $350 and took seven months to design, create and install in 1938. The entire project of funding and commissioning forty-four (44) stained glass windows took almost three decades, overseen by various figures at St. Ignatius. Most of the Triforium windows were commissioned by Fr. Ward from 1940-1945. Fr. Carroll M. O'Sullivan, S.J., and Fr. William Tobin, S.J. oversaw eighteen (18) clerestory windows and five (5) first balcony windows. The Mary Magdalen window was the final stained glass piece to be installed in the church in 1963. This window was created under the direction of Rector Fr. Charles Dullea, S.J.

Eighteen Circular Windows (4'3" diameter)

The windows are listed in the order they appear from the entrance of the church moving towards the main altar. The date the windows were completed has been included. Click here for a description of each of the individual windows in the publication "Symbolism of the Stained Glass Windows: Saint Ignatius Church" written by John C. Ward, S.J. in 1944.

RIGHT SIDE	LEFT SIDE
St. Francis of Assisi, 1942	St. Isaac Jogues, 1941
St. Cecilia, 1941	St. Thomas Aquinas, 1941
St. Peter Canisius, 1941	St. Andrew Bobola,
St. John Berchmans, 1941	St. Stanislaus Kostka, 1941
St. Ives, 1938	St. Joseph, 1940
St. Ignatius of Loyola, 1941	Blessed Virgin Mary, 1940
St. Augustine, 1939	St. Robert Bellarmine, 1941
St. Francis Xavier, 1942	Sacred Heart, 1940
St. Alphonsus Rodriguez, 1940	St. Aloysius, 1940

Large Clerestory Windows (17' high x 5'4" wide)

The windows are listed in the order they appear from the entrance of the church moving towards the main altar. The original descriptions for the majority of the windows can be viewed by clicking here.

RIGHT SIDE	LEFT SIDE
St. Esther, 1958	Mary Magdalene, 1962
Isaiah the Prophet, 1956	St. Matthias, 1962
St. James the Lesser, 1955	St. Simon, 1952

MARBLE ALTAR, SANCTUARY, BALDACCHINO, ALTAR RAILINGS

When the church first opened, the Jesuits had no funds for a new altar to match the magnificence of the basilica. So they had students carry the "temporary wooden altar" from "the temporary church" on Hayes Street. Father Terrence Mahan, SJ, in his master's thesis on St. Ignatius Church under Father McGloin's direction, wrote about an "undersized wooden altar in an oversized unpainted church on an unfinished sanctuary floor" as a definite deficiency. During the depression and the war, Father William Dunne, president of USF and religious superior of the Jesuit community, managed to keep the school afloat, but there were no extra funds for the church during those years. However, once enrollments skyrocketed after the war, he, Father James Lyons, and Mr. and Mrs. Charles Harney worked with historical pictures from the Hayes Street church and commissioned an Italian marble floor for both the lower and upper sanctuary, full marble altar rails around all of the altars, a high altar with a grand tabernacle and tall marble candelabra in scale and resonance with the building's architecture. In many respects, the design surpassed the pre-1906 church, especially with the stunning surprise of the wooden baldacchino (canopy) of white Appalachian oak from Lacrosse, Wisconsin to match the sanctuary doors. The 3000 square foot area is white rectangles of Calacatta marble (Italian cremo) with black rectangles of Poorto Venere, with Roos Levant boarders and baseboards of Verde Alpio. By the 1949 Centennial of the Jesuits' arrival in San Francisco, the altar and sanctuary were finally congruent with the rest of the church.

The weight of the new sanctuary necessitated reinforcing the church foundations in 1949. After the 1989 earthquake, the church's steel structure proved sound. However, since the marble sanctuary was a later addition, unanticipated in the original design, this is the one area of the church that required additional seismic work.

THE BAPTISMAL CHAPEL

The Blaettler Family commissioned the conversion of a storage room in the back vestibule into a proper baptismal chapel in memory of Peter Blaettler and John-Paul Calegari. In addition to the two della Robbia works, the inner chapel has a unique work showing Ignatius' vision at the chapel of La Storta. In this work, Ignatius is greeted by Christ carrying the cross with God the Father and the Holy Spirit alongside Him. God the Father tells Ignatius, "I will be with you in Rome" before Ignatius met with the Pope to form the Society of Jesus.

THE RECONCILATION CHAPEL

After the Second Vatican Council, different forms of the sacrament of reconciliation were encouraged, one of which included a face to face arrangement, similar to traditional spiritual direction. Father Gagan, the pastor, approached the Ed Clougherty Family in 1995, then commissioned Ed Sabini to design the chapel using parts of the wooden confessionals as decorations. The key feature is a Padaraino art work showing the Prodigal Son returning to the waiting arms of his father. This image dominates both the interior and exterior of the reconciliation chapel.

A special Examen Prayer area donated by a Greek Orthodox Catholic family, the Boosalis family, whose six children attended St. Ignatius College Prep, contains several special icons of Christ as a perfect meditation before the sacrament of reconciliation.

THE SACRISTY

The sacristy of St. Ignatius Church was enriched after the 1915 World's Fair, the Panama-Pacific Exposition, with several hand-carved wooden chests and cabinets designed and carved in the Jesuit Orphanage of Ziukawei near Shaghai. They were sent from China for the Fair, and the US government granted permission for the Jesuits to retain them in the US as long as they were not sold. The pieces were distributed to most of the Jesuit communities in the Province.

The left side of the sacristy area for over 100 years served as the Sanctuary Society robing room with a series of wooden lockers. The cassocks and surplices hung on hooks, while the lockers were for the young men's coats, sweaters, and school books. For years the locks worked as a preventative against theft; however, the locks did not prevent pranks. When a newly assigned freshman would turn his back to hang up his jacket, it was not unusual for the older boys to "stuff" him into a locker and turn the key. Jesuit scholastics got tired of hearing the cries of "detained" altar boys during Mass. Eventually, the locks were ornamental rather than functional. The circular area behind the altar provides storage church decorations, candelabra, banners, vases, pilasters, and additional kneelers.

THE ART GALLERY

Starting in the 1990s, the backside areas of the church feature special displays of liturgical art, some of which go back to the church on Van Ness Avenue. The large tapestry processional banner of the Gentleman's sodality, which has an embroidery of Our Lady on one side and of St. Ignatius Loyola on the other, dates from the late 1800's. It is brought out each year for the feast of St. Ignatius (July 31) and other special occasions. During the construction of the church a special mahogany wood cabinet was built for the banner in the anteroom in the east steeple of St. Ignatius Church. In the 1990's, on the advice of a conservator, the banner was placed in a more suitable case, at a 45-degree angle to preserve it from deterioration. The cabinet which formerly held the banner now contains a full-length mirror which is used by brides and the attendants preparing for their wedding. The brass frame which holds the banner in processions is stored along the wall next to the sacristy door closest to the main altar.

1953
A ROADBLOCK TO REDECORATION -- PARTIAL ROOF AND MAJOR MASONRY REPAIR

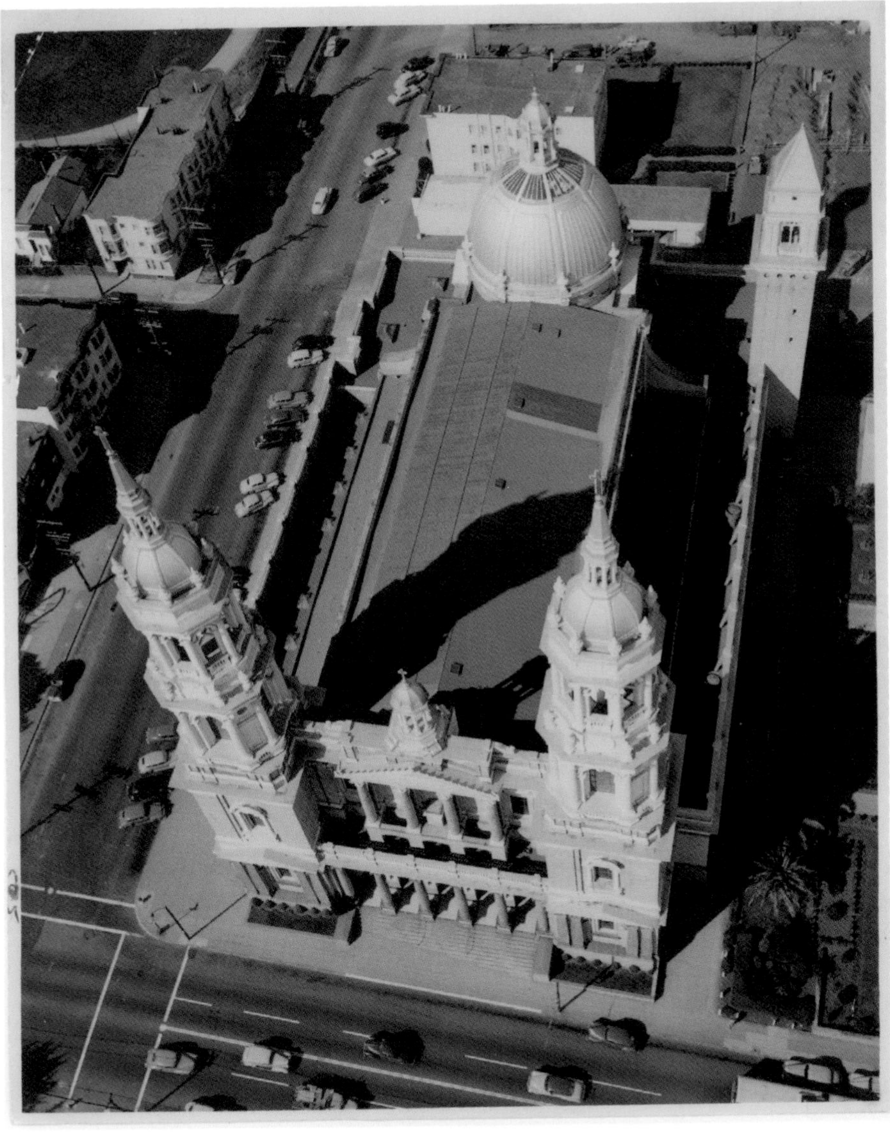

In 1914, someone painted graffiti on the inside of the exterior dome – "this dome leaks!" That "original and innovative" iron metal roof did not "last a lifetime" – in fact, it did not make it through the first winter. It was not unusual for congregants to continue wearing rain coats during Mass since "raindrops kept falling on their heads." Congregants soon learned to walk to the sink in the back vestibule, grab one of the many flower pots, and carefully place it on a pew to catch the leakage. Every morning after 5am Mass, altar boys were assigned to empty the pots and place them back again.

After 40 years of attaching new gutters and applying patches, the pots and barrels could no longer contain the problem. Finally, rust stains began to form "maps" on the unpainted plaster walls and pillars. In 1953 Father Francis Seeliger, SJ, decided to call in roofing and structural engineers to study the problem. Father McGloin reported that outside repair work became "virtually impossible for there was not sufficient metal left for the patching process," so the entire roof would have to be replaced. However, further inspection revealed damage to the church's rust jackets around the steel framing. This involved major masonry repair on the cornices and the dome. If one studies the towers and the Parker Street sides corners of the church, one can see the partial repair work where the brick masonry is slightly off.

All the metal on the east tower was renewed and painted as was the metal on the west tower above the brickwork. But to complete the project properly, Father Seeliger estimated the cost at $124,000 ($1,283,880 in today's dollars). Due to the lack of funds, the renovation of the brickwork was not completed at that time. In fact, it has never been completed to this day and has become a major concern for the structural integrity of the building.

There were no funds left over to paint over the rust stains on the interior plaster, so those stains remained for another 10 years. Sadly, the flower pots to catch rain water multiplied through the late 1950s -- congregants knew which pews to avoid during rainstorms. Instead of redesigning the roof, impossible given the fact that there are 12 different roof sections, a series of pipes and scupper drains was installed and requires periodic replacement due to deterioration from the salt air and fog. For years, the Jesuit Brother who served as the church sacristan would have to climb several flights of stairs to the area surrounding the dome and empty the buckets filled with rain water after each major storm.

1962-1964 INTERNAL DECORATION FOR GOLDEN JUBILEE

As the 50th anniversary for the church approached, the Jesuits realized that the original design to paint and decorate the interior still remained unfinished; further, the external niche above the entrance intended for a statue of St. Ignatius remained empty save for the pigeons who nested there. The original lighting system, state of the art for 1914, had become antiquated and inadequate. In 1962 Father Charles Dullea, SJ commissioned the Conrad Schmidt School of Milwaukee, Wisconsin to complete the original interior decoration of the church for the Golden Jubilee. This project commenced in the summer of 1962 and involved the installation of scaffolding for each of the side sections, then eventually for the main nave area. During services, the artists lay flat on their backs to apply gold leaf by hand, sometimes invoking God's name in a "different" prayer than those in the approved missal.

For two years, the church took on the appearance of the Sistine Chapel under Michelangelo's brushes. The design with all the various gradations of colors – rich creams, light and dark greys, pale and bright whites, and brilliant gold leaf details was more sophisticated than anyone imagined. If one got distracted during an unusually long homily, one could observe the application of gold leaf and paint on the ceiling, the pilasters, the columns, and the "gingerbread" that adorned the arches. Once the first side sections were completed, congregants could see the full effect and marveled. They affectionately nicknamed the church "Father Dullea's Fox Theatre" after the famed movie palace on Market Street, but on completion students later dubbed the edifice that 'The Jebbie Opera House."

The cost of the interior decoration, which also involved a partial roof repair was $100,000. The entire Jesuit communities of the high school and the university celebrated the church's Golden Anniversary on Sunday, September 20, 1964 -- 52 years after placement of the cornerstone and the original architect envisioned the interior design. Finally, all of the stained- glass windows, the shrines, the side altars, and the gold leaf flourishes were completed. Even a statue of St. Ignatius finally took its place on the niche above the main entrance.

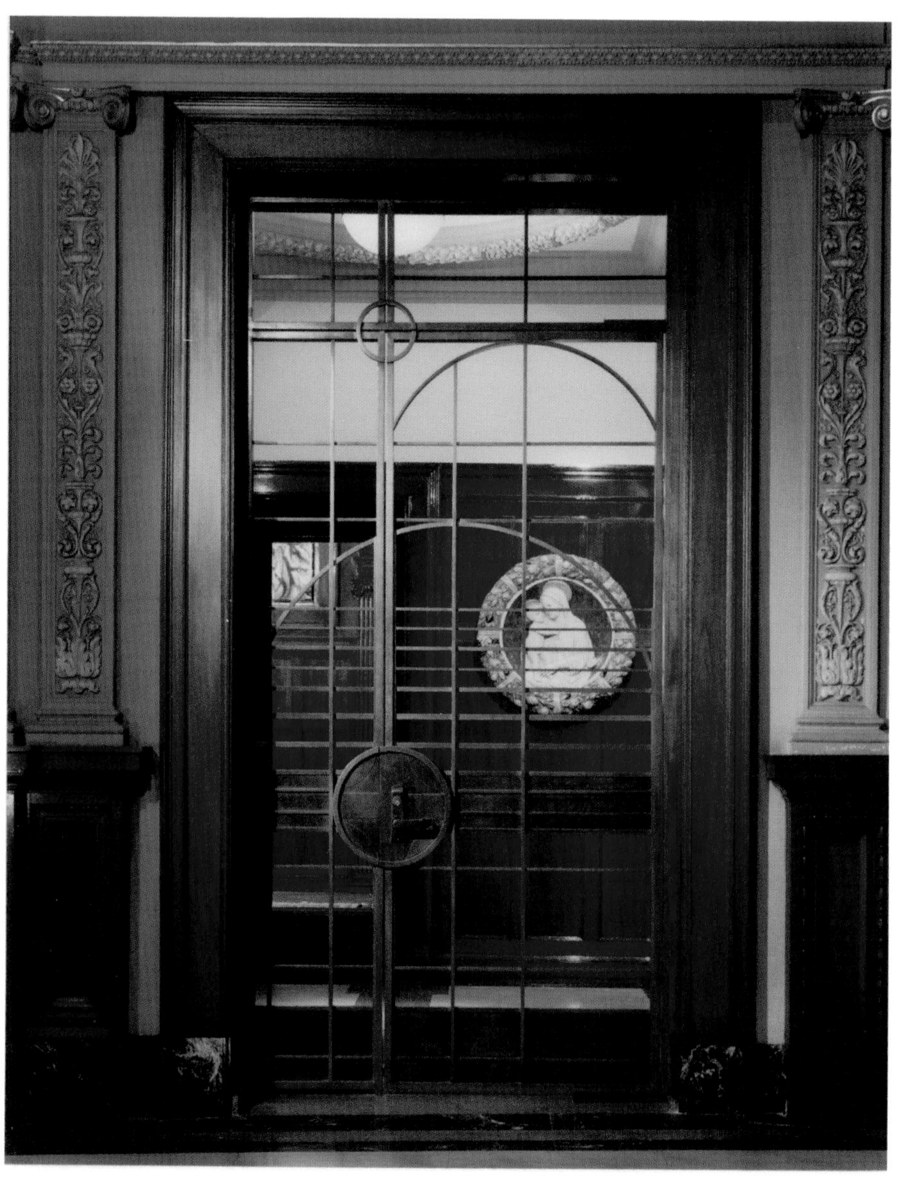

THE PETER BLAETTLER / JOHN-PAUL CALEGARI BAPTISMAL CHAPEL

THE BOOSALIS FAMILY ICON PRAYER CHAPEL

OUR LADY OF GUADALUPE CHAPEL

SACRED HEART CHAPEL

ST. ALPHONSUS RODRIGUEZ CHAPEL

ST. ANTHONY OF PADUA SHRINE

ST. FRANCIS XAVIER CHAPEL

ST. IGNATIUS SHRINE

ST. JOSEPH ALTAR

ST. PETER CANISIUS CHAPEL

ST. ROBERT BELLARMINE CHAPEL

IGNATIUS LOYOLA SHRINE AT THE BACK OF THE CHURCH

Chapter Six

TALES FROM THE CRYPT:

THE CRYPT ALTARS:

Bill Hogan '55 recalls his days in the sanctuary society in the 1950s. "In my memory, it was huge, dimly lit, and spooky. The crypt was under the main altar, the space equivalent to the size of the sanctuary above it. There must have been at least a dozen altars. I remember them as being around the outer circular wall. We had 12 faculty priests at SI in '55, and USF had 35, plus the retired and infirm, and those who ministered to SI church. They each said private masses every day. SI church was not a parish at that time, but the church was staffed with its own priests, confessionals were manned every morning, mass on the main altar every hour from 6 to 9. We altar boys used the sacristy on the west side of the sanctuary, to vest in cassock and surplice, and there was a door opening onto the stairway that went down to the crypt. Liturgy was in Latin, facing the wall."

Once Xavier Hall chapel – with 10 side chapels – opened in 1959, the crypt altars fell into disuse. After the 1989 earthquake, retrofitting the sanctuary closed the crypt permanently. The only room left is the Arrupe Room.

MAD MARY

Because each priest in the Jesuit community had to say daily Mass, and because there were over 92 priests in the combined high school and university communities in the 1940s and 1950s, it was necessary to have a substantial number of Masses each morning and an equally substantial number of altars. Therefore, the first Masses of the day would begin at 5:15am, with 9 priests celebrating at the same time – one at the main altar, and 8 others at the side altars.

Since there was a special indulgence to attending multiple Masses on the same day, one infamous nurse from St. Mary's hospital – with great reverence and devotion – would position herself in the last pew in the center right aisle where she could have a view of all 9 altars. When the consecration bells would ring for each altar, she would quickly scurry over to bless herself, then quickly change directions when the next bell would ring for another consecration. It was not unusual to see her running from altar to altar in a mad dash for indulgences.

The altar boys – and some Jesuits – nicknamed her Mad Mary, since Mary was her first name.

OUTDOOR MASS DURING 1918 FLU EPIDEMIC

DECEMBER 31, 1931
FIREFIGHTERS SAVE ST IGNATIUS CHURCH

Two hours after the Te Deum New Year's Eve service, an electrical fire broke out in the roof area above the choir loft. Because of the location, firefighters had to cut open a passage above the organ loft to reach the blaze, working 80 feet above the main floor. One of the firemen, Florence Scannell, climbed through the makeshift opening and dragged heavy hoses behind him. Suddenly, the adjacent ceiling panel gave way and Scannell and his captain, William Taylor, fell forty feet to the organ loft. Both were rushed to nearby St. Mary's hospital, while the remaining crew extinguished the fire and saved the church. New Year's Day Scannell died of his injuries. Joseph Cronan donated funds for the repairs and a memorial plaque (next to the door leading the main altar) in honor of Scannell and the firefighters who saved St. Ignatius Church.

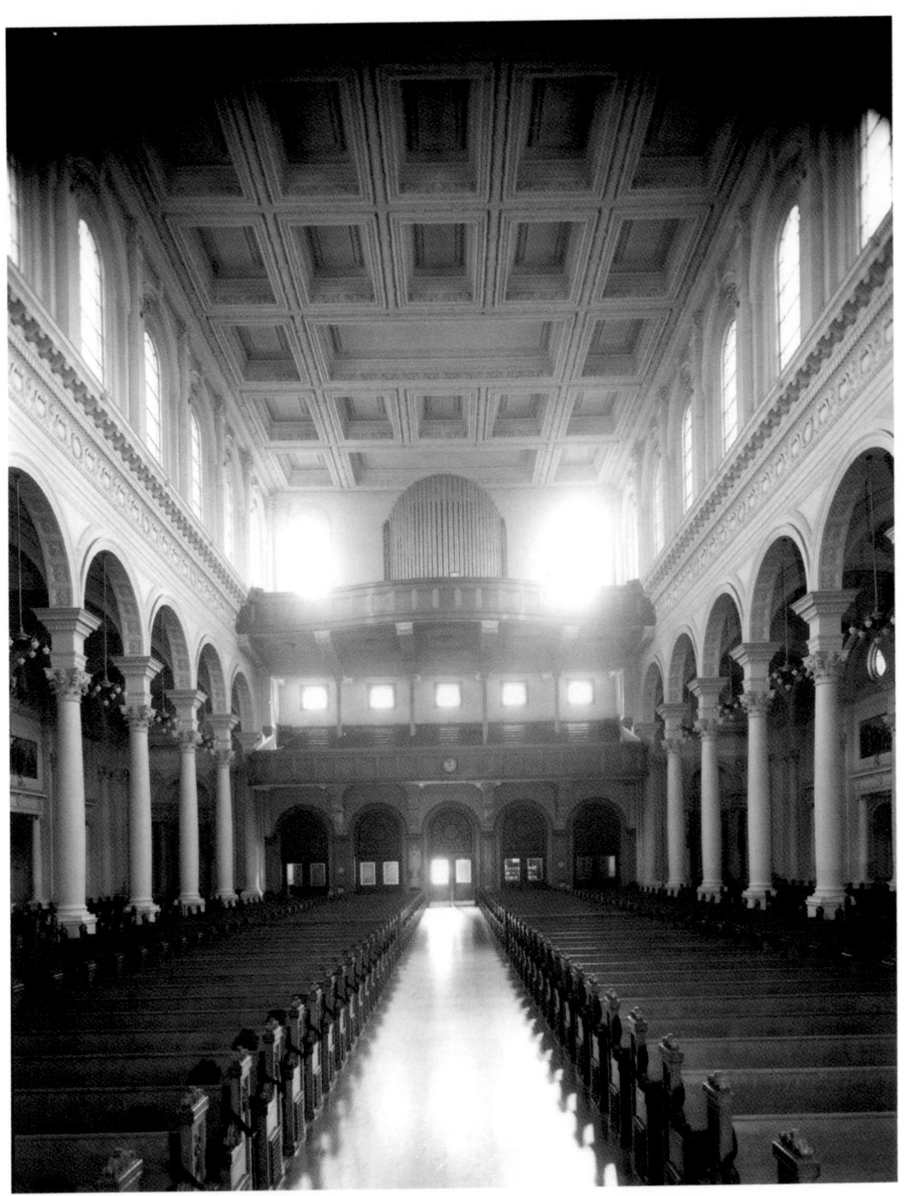

THE UNPAINTED CHURCH BEFORE THE ORGAN PIPES WERE MOVED

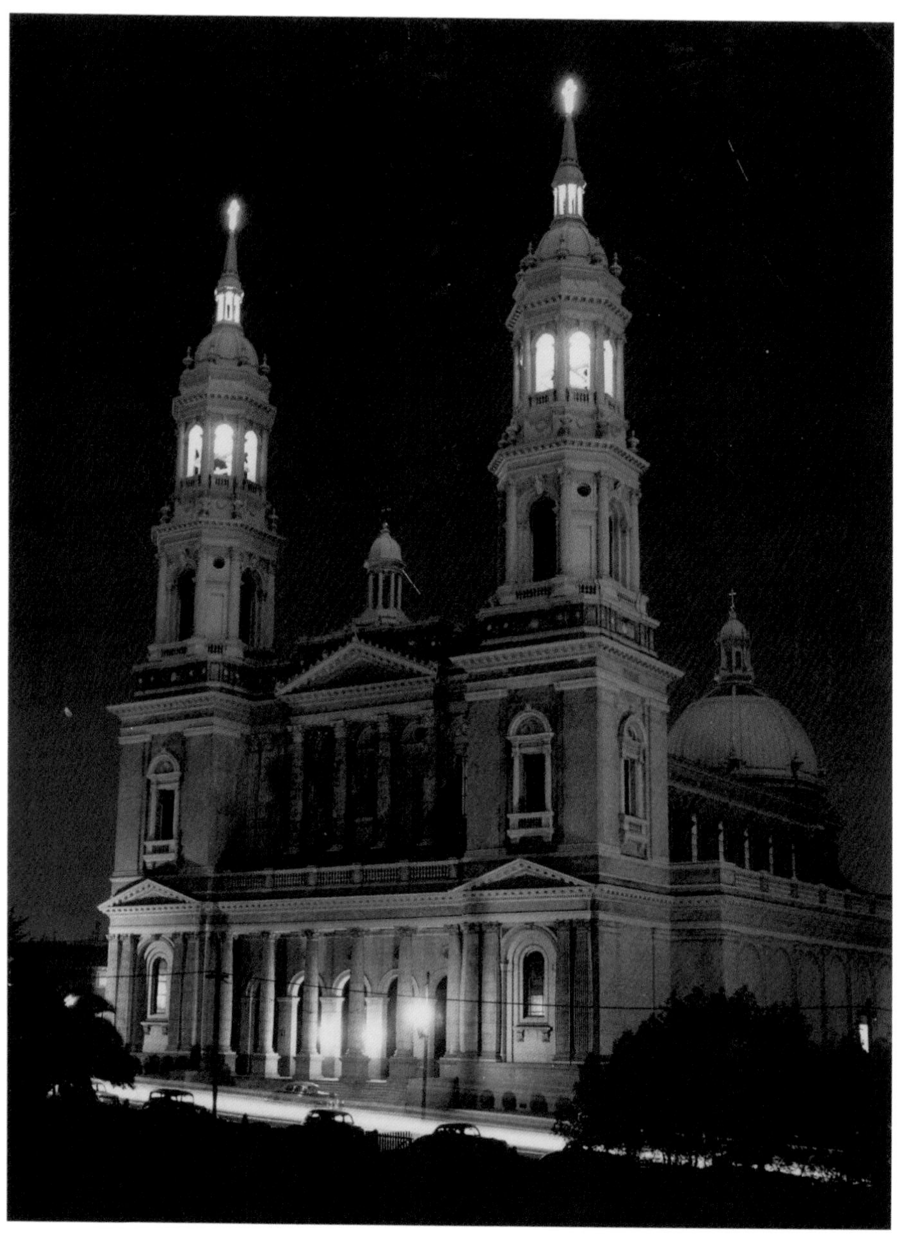

1960 SI CHURCH AT NIGHT WITH THE GREEN NEON CROSSES TO ALERT AIRPLANES

Once airplanes took to the skies above San Francisco, the church – the tallest landmark in the city – required illumination of its towers. During the late 1920s little light bulbs outlined the two crosses atop the towers; eventually, the interior of the towers were illuminated and green neon outlined the two crosses to warn planes away from the church and the nearby Twin Peaks, Mount Sutro, and Lone Mountain. Old timers recalled Father Neri's illumination of the Market Street towers back in 1876 where the towers of St. Ignatius blazed in the night sky above San Francisco.

THE 12:15 KEZAR/49ER MASS IN THE 1950S AND 1960S

Once San Francisco acquired a professional football team, the 49ers, Sunday football games packed Kear stadium, 4 blocks from St. Ignatius Church. The football franchise, in deference to the City's large Catholic population, delayed game time until 2pm. So Sunday's 12:15 Mass had to end before 1pm not just so that the fans in the congregation could get to the game, but so the ushers could. Many ushers at St. Ignatius Church were also ushers and ticket takers at Kezar Stadium. Further, the high school Fathers' Club used to sell parking spaces in the high school playground to subsidize scholarships. The 12:15 Mass became popular not only with 49ers fans, but with the general congregation during the football season -- it promised eloquent, but brief preaching.

PAGING FATHER ANTHONY MARASCHI, SJ

For years behind the switchboard operator at the Jesuit's Xavier Hall residence hung a picture of what appeared to be an old-time country priest in black cassock wearing an Italian Beretta cap with his hands folded over his rosary beads. For years no one who visited the residence knew the name of this simple Jesuit except USF's resident historian Father John McGloin who would carefully explain that this simple priest accomplished mighty things – he was a true San Francisco pioneer: Father Anthony Maraschi, founder of St. Ignatius.

When nursing students on scholarship were hired as switchboard operators at Xavier Hall, an infamous prank was for members of the College Players, the theatre society, to call the switchboard on a Friday night and ask to speak to Father Maraschi. When the switchboard operator could not locate a Father Maraschi in the community, the prankster would claim Father was a highly respected Italian theologian, would need the guest suite, and would arrive from SF airport within the hour. In desperation, the student operator would call the Jesuit minister to reserve a room for Father Maraschi, only to be informed by Father McGloin, "My God, madam, he's been dead for 75 years."

In 1985, a bronze bust of Father Maraschi was commissioned from local artist Harriet Moore; it stands on the lawn behind the hilltop church, just behind the cornerstone for the 1880 church.

THIS IS A PICTURE OF THE ANNUAL VETERANS DAY MILITARY MASS WHEN ALL USF STUDENTS TOOK MANDATORY ROTC TRAINING FOR THEIR FIRST TWO YEARS.

At the annual Military Mass, the Flag with stars for all of St. Ignatius' deceased military vets hung behind the main altar. This picture was taken in the 1944 during World War II.

THE COSTLIEST PENANCE EVER ADMINSITERED

An infamous, but true story involves a priest in the confessional and a woman who frequented the sacrament weekly. She always appeared simply dressed in modest clothing, not exactly a bag lady, but not someone who attended Sunday Mass with white gloves, hat and matching purse. One day she expressed her desire to make a "little donation" to the Jesuit Fathers. Father, assuming her donation would indeed be small, and knowing the impoverished state of the Carmelite Sisters across the street, suggested that his penitent consider giving her "little donation" to the "good Sisters." And she did – over a million dollars! The Sisters abandoned their simple wooden structure and built the beautiful convent and chapel directly across the street from St. Ignatius – eternally grateful for the thoughtfulness of the Jesuit fathers.

The Carmelite Monastery of Christo Rey still has an audio speaker in their monastery connected to the St. Ignatius Church sound system so the cloistered sisters hear the homilies, liturgies and other activities of St. Ignatius. (as one Jesuit put it: you get our donation, you listen to our homilies!)

CHRISMAS DECORATIONS - A MARVEL OF ENGINEERING

Using photographs from the pre-1906 church, in 1994 parishioners decided to decorate the church at Christmas with garlands encircling the pillars and a forest of trees behind the altar. For Easter, the tabernacle altar and marble stairs, the Altar of Sacrifice, Mary and Joseph's shrines, and the high pulpit were adorned with a field of Easter Lilies. Advent, Christmas and Easter decorations make the church a special destination for visitors and tourists. However, the process often puzzles Mass goers as their eyes scan the advent wreath or the pillar garlands – how are the decorations hung at such dizzying heights?

To hang the advent wreath, the USF Plant Services installed a set of four wires and pulleys in the spacious access area below the upper roof but above the ornamental ceiling. The wires are so carefully hidden that the wreath seems to float in space. Before Advent the wires are lowered, and the wreath is linked to the wires and centered and balanced by a team of USF plant services workers using a power lift and/or scaffolding.

The garlands and wreaths are hung using a system devised by retired St. Ignatius church artisan Phil Caswell. He taught parish volunteers and USF Plant Services how to use a power lift and wrap the garland around the columns in a specific way. The wreaths are strung between columns by means of wires stored at the tops of each column. The workers use a power lift to do this and plug the wreaths' lights into electric power cords which are also stored at the top of each columns. Similarly, seasonal banners are hung using the powerlift and have become a new addition to the liturgical seasons.

UNUSUAL IN THE DAY TO DAY SACRISTAN'S JOB

In the 1990's the sacristan saw a man standing on a stool who had attached tracing paper to trace the outline of the figures onto the paper. When the sacristan went over to inquire, he realized the man was wearing a priest's cassock. The priest explained his church in Mexico had been destroyed in a fire, so he was tracing out the art work in St. Ignatius Church in order to recreate the painting's figures for his church which was in the process of being rebuilt.

Around the year 2000 a very well dressed and elegant yet slightly disturbed woman, had a habit of lighting all the votive candles at all the side altars. The sacristan approached her after several days and politely requested that she "leave some for others."

"Don't worry, I will pay for them" she added and continued to light the candles. A few days later a distinguished looking older man introduced himself at the St. Ignatius Church office as the caretaker for the woman; he apologized and said it would not happen again.

Entering the church one morning about two weeks later, the sacristan discovered a pile of papers on the main altar – a large number of $50 dollars bills neatly fanned out across the altar, totaling $2,950.00. He looked around and saw no one in the church but immediately thought of what the woman had said about paying for the candles. He brought the money to the parish business manager with the suggestion it be at least partially used for the Mission Dolores Academy which the parish had begun to support.

UP INTO THE IGNATIAN HEIGHTS

Just as the Jesuit sacristan would have to ascend six flights of stairs to empty the water buckets, the altar boys would often ascend the same staircases, almost always without sanction, to roam around the catwalks above the false ceiling. A tradition was to inscribe one's name on the walls. One could also go out the doors leading to the roofs above the side altars for a spectacular view of the campus, the ocean, and downtown. Members of the church staff still use this as their vantage point for the annual flight of the Blue Angels on Fleet Week. Some altar boys were even courageous enough to ascend the eastern tower up to the top opening, but pigeons had long since claimed the territory as their domain, so the errant altar boy discovered the stain of his sin rather quickly and beat a hasty retreat.

Similarly, a group of young men would tour the towers by ascending five staircases to the original choir loft, then up the additional three flights to the base of the eastern tower. At this junction one could cross over to the western tower or continue up into the lower part of the spire, ascend the spiral staircase – dodging disgruntled pigeons and stepping around years of pigeon droppings – to the second cupula. The view was dazzling and dizzying. When the towers were lighted and repaired in the 1980s, mesh prevented the pigeons from nesting in the tower areas.

BABY JESUS KIDNAPPED, FOUND COMFORTING A HOMELESS MAN OUTSIDE STARBUCKS

For the first 75 years, the Christmas nativity scene was set up in front of St Joseph's Altar with a beautiful sky background painted by the College Players stage crew. Dramatic lighting highlighted the beauty of the century old figurines, and the Christmas Crib became a destination during the holiday season.

With the addition of the 4pm Christmas Eve Family Liturgy, the need for a different location became necessary, so Father Gagan chose the alcove over by the Parker Street entrance. Now the nativity set became another side altar shrine during the season which attracted children especially.

No one worried about the safety of the figurines when they were at Joseph's altar since the altar railing easily created a barrier. However, the Parker Street site had no boundary – adventurous unsupervised children could easily climb in and join Jesus. Most parents were super careful not to have this happen.

But one morning congregants discovered the Baby Jesus was no longer in his manger. A witty homilist asked the congregants to keep their eyes out for the missing infant statue -- it was too early for the feast of the Holy Family's Flight to Egypt.

A few hours later a USF Public Safety officer stopped for coffee at Starbucks in Laurel Village and saw a homeless man sitting on the sidewalk with a statue of the Baby Jesus alongside him. The sweet picture of the baby Jesus comforting a homeless man touched the officer. Since the statue did not have a ransom note attached, he called Maureen Corrigan at the parish, then drove her down to identify and reclaim the baby Jesus. But first they ministered the immediate needs of the homeless man. When they restored the infant to the manger, the figurine only showed some minor effects of marking-pen graffiti.

Now when the children set the Baby Jesus in his nativity setting as part of the 4pm Christmas Eve Mass, the sacristan steals back after Mass to safety chain Jesus down – much like a parent would in a baby's car set -- just for safe keeping.

To this day, neither the sacristan nor any of the priests could figure out what Baby Jesus wanted at Starbucks.

Around the same time period, locks were installed on the confessional doors since the church became a favored location for homeless squatters. They would hide in the confessional until after the church was locked, then sleep in the pews. For their own safety and the safety of the church building, campus security urged the church to install locks on the confessional doors when not in use for the actual sacrament.

THE CROSS CLOSES PARKER AVENUE

While the church structure survived the 1989 World Series Quake, the cross on the western tower tilted towards Parker Avenue. Finally, a storm loosened the cross and it fell into a precarious position where it could easily fall to the ground and impale students and parishioners. Because the cross was entangled in its own tower – close to 15 stories above ground – fire department ladders could not reach the height. For a week, Parker Avenue had to be closed until a special crane could be brought across the Golden Gate Bridge from Marin. The day the crane arrived, so did a sizable audience, including several local news crews. Fortunately, after several failed attempts, the worker was able to lean out "just a few more inches" to grab the cross and prevent it – and himself – from flying through the air to the crowd below. When the towers were repaired several years later, both crosses were specially secured to prevent a repetition.

Chapter Seven

QUAKES – THE COUNCIL, THE GENERAL CONGREGATION, THE COUNTERCULTURE 1965-1989

FIRST QUAKE – THE COUNCIL AND THE COUNTER CULTURE CHANGE 1966-72

If one took a snapshot of the congregation attending a typical mid-1960s Sunday Mass, the older men wore business suits, the younger men wore blue blazers and slacks, but all sported dress shirts and ties, dark socks and dress shoes, and neat haircuts. After genuflecting on entrance to the pews, the men would click the catch button to hold their hats. Women wore either Jackie Kennedy-style pastel suits or Audrey Hepburn-style black or beige dresses, all hems skimmed the knees, and nylons, high heels, matching purses, and black, beige or white gloves completed the ensemble. Due to the cold weather, stylish cloth coats had only the best labels from I. Magnin's, City of Paris, the White House or other fashionable stores. Women's hats had mostly shrunk to the smaller pillbox hats fashionable in the Kennedy White House, though one could pick up a veil or left-over gloves on the back table if need be. These "Sunday Best" clothes also served for going shopping downtown, attending the Curran or Geary theatres, visiting the doctors at 450 Sutter or 490 Post, or even attending a first-class movie at the Fox or the Warfield. San Franciscans were formal dressers, especially for Sunday church services.

During the early 1960s St. Ignatius Church played host to many traditional formal liturgies. In addition to the high school and college's Masses of the Holy Spirit or graduations, every First Friday the high school students would march up the hill single file in black suits, white dress shirts, red or blue school-colored ties, and black leather dress shoes. The high school and university were not alone in offering formal liturgies during that time period. After St. Mary's Cathedral on Van Ness burned down, St. Ignatius was chosen to host ordinations, major Catholic funerals, and yearly Masses for the Thomas More Society of lawyers and judges, as well as the Police and Fire Departments.

After the Vatican Council adjourned in 1965, after the Civil Rights and Vietnam War Protests, and after the Summer of Love, the City – and St. Ignatius Church -- experienced a cultural earthquake. The Council Fathers decided to allow for vernacular liturgy, so the new English Mass gradually rolled in over a two-year period from 1965-67. Another major reform was turning the altar around so the priest could face the people; and a further change was allowing for liturgical music with contemporary instruments, not just traditional organ music. St. Ignatius Church not only adapted to many of these changes in creative ways, but often took the lead in implementation.

The Jesuit community educated the congregations about the new English Mass, and they chose popular preachers to gradually introduce the changes, particularly Father Charles Dullea, Father Edward Stackpoole, and Father Steven Early. The church maintained traditional Latin for most of the prayers at the 5:30, 6:15, 7:15 and 8:15 services in respect for those older congregations' preferences; but the later Masses quickly implemented the liturgical reforms to receptive congregations. Eventually, all Masses were in English, but only the later ones employed music.

In 1967, the university's campus ministry department instituted more informal Masses in the University Center Lounge at 10:30 on Sunday mornings, and the congregations for this new Folk Mass grew so large that the university claimed one of the Sunday time slots. The university commissioned a wooden altar so the priest could face the people, moved in a grand piano, and introduced microphones for the folk ensemble. In fall of 1969, Father Elliott Short, SJ, the campus minister, invited composer Vince Guaraldi, famous for his musical scores for the *Peanuts*' television specials, to compose and perform a Jazz Mass.

By 1968, a radical change occurred in the congregations -- no more hats, gloves, suits, ties, high heels and dress shoes. Not only did college students come to Mass in casual clothing, so did the adults -- khakis, sports shirts, sweaters, casual dresses, even sweats, athletic shoes, and Levis. The formal high school First Friday Masses "went casual," keeping the dress shirt and tie, but allowing for school jackets and block club sweaters.

The Jesuits at St. Ignatius Church adapted to change in creative ways. So as not to disrupt many traditional Catholics, the church continued to offer a 6:30am Sunday Mass which served the nurses and doctors at St. Mary's hospital as well as police and firemen working at City Hall and the Hall of Justice. However, the infrequently attended 5:30am Mass disappeared from the schedule since there was no longer a fast from midnight in order to receive the Eucharist.

The great tradition of Jesuit preaching continued to flourish, but for the contemporary Masses the preacher often would often abandon the high pulpit and stand in front of the altar to be closer to the congregation. When the diocese stopped the evening Youth

Liturgy at St Mary's Cathedral, St. Ignatius picked up many who frequented that liturgy, and soon the 4pm Sunday Mass acquired an overflowing congregation of young people from all over the city.

The Jesuits tailored each Sunday Mass for distinct congregations. The 6:30am and 8am congregations, older and more traditional, were uninterested in singing the parts of the liturgy, so these eventually became the "quiet" liturgies. The 9:30am Mass became the youth and family liturgy with contemporary folk music, and the 11am liturgy employed a traditional choir with classical music from the Latin and Gregorian music heritage. The vigil Mass on Saturday had a mixture of traditional and contemporary musical styles.

In 1969 the high school moved to its new campus in the Sunset, closing one chapter in the church's history – gone was the altar server society and those First Friday Masses. A second marker of change was when Father John McGloin published the first history of St. Ignatius Church *Jesuits by the Golden Gate* in 1972 with monthly installments in the church bulletin that captured the nostalgia, but noted the end of an era.

SI BECOMES THE CATHOLIC SCHOOL GRADUATION DESTINATION

Even though St. Ignatius Church could not celebrate weddings or baptisms, the church has always been the destination for elaborate graduations. Since the church was the largest assembly hall except for Civic Auditorium until the new St. Mary's Cathedral opened, it was not unusual for several Catholic high schools to book the church.

Since the church first opened in 1914, St. Ignatius College Prep held either Baccalaureate Mass or Graduation in St. Ignatius Church. Over 25,000 graduates have "walked the aisle" and out the doors with the city laying at their feet, a favorite line for valedictorians. Brother Douglas Draper, dean of St. Ignatius College Prep for over 40 years, became famous for the class, dignity and respect of his graduation ceremonies. Several of the women's Catholic high schools also graduated from St. Ignatius -- Presentation Academy, Notre Dame Belmont, and Mercy Burlingame. On the 100th anniversary of the Schools of the Sacred Heart in San Francisco, the celebratory Mass was held at St. Ignatius Church.

While the University celebrated a Baccalaureate Mass twice annually in December and May, for years graduations were held off campus at either the Opera House or Civic Auditorium. However, Father John LoSchiavo, decided to break up the graduation ceremonies by colleges which allowed for several "mini" graduation services that are now held in the church. It is not unusual on graduation weekend for one group to assemble outside the church on Welch Hall lawn while another graduation marched out the Fulton Street doors.

THE SECOND QUAKE – A GENERAL CONGREGATION ENHANCES THE MISSION 1972 - 1985

When it seemed that the culture quakes were over with, a new one gently rocked the entire Jesuit world. When the Jesuit representatives from the worldwide provinces gathered in Rome to elect Father Pedro Arrupe, SJ as Superior General, General Congregation 34 issued new directives for Jesuit apostolates, especially a renewal of administering the Spiritual Exercises for not only Jesuits but lay persons.

At St. Ignatius Church, the changes again were gradual. Many Jesuit priests became regular spiritual directors for lay Catholics, offering a form of the Spiritual Exercises Ignatius had used on the first companions at the University of Paris – the 19th Annotation of the Spiritual Exercises. This allowed people with active lives to complete the retreat in the midst of their work and family life schedules. The 19th Annotation retreat proved especially popular with younger Catholics, so St. Ignatius Church often became the unofficial parish for many post-college Catholics and their young families.

With the rush of many families to the suburbs in the mid and late 1970s, the size of congregations at churches all over the City declined, and St. Ignatius experienced a fall-off in attendance. The reduction in collections created a financial crisis since maintenance of the church had to be borne by the university. But the Jesuit community faced more major handicap dating back to 1915 -- the dome still leaked.

Through the years, various solutions had been applied and failed, including an extensive system of plastic tubes which circled the inside of the dome to catch the leaks. Roofers called it a band-aid solution, one of the Jesuits called it “a band-aid on a corpse non-solution.” The series of additional gutters and the patch job on the towers was giving way to the salt air elements on the Hilltop.

In 1985 with the arrival of Father Charles Gagan, the church acquired its best guardian since Father Dullea. A former high school president and chaplain, he possessed the perfect combination of skills – he implemented the new pastoral and social justice programs mandated by the General Congregations of the Society of Jesus. As a former altar boy and young scholastic, he knew the maintenance needs of the church, so he created a team to launch a fund-raising campaign.

PGE approached the Jesuits with an unusual proposition. The utility considered St. Ignatius Church a major City landmark – they cited the twin spires at the heart of the City as a beacon of hope after the 1906 earthquake and fire. They wanted to use the landmark church as a pilot project. They proposed to design and assume the cost for an external lighting system for the entire building, not just the twin spires, so that St. Ignatius would standout against the night sky along with the Golden Gate Bridge.

A week before a "Celebration of Light" event to show off the new lighting, a 6.9 earthquake struck the entire Northern California region, even stopping the Bay Area World Series. Freeways collapsed, apartment buildings pancaked, and fires broke out in the Marina; most of the city was blanketed in darkness while PGE inspectors went city block by city block for safety checks before restoring power. Since the inspectors started at the ocean and worked their way across the city, St. Ignatius was the first major structure to receive power. Ironically, several days prior to the schedule lighting, St. Ignatius Church provided the city with a Celebration of Light that signaled "all safe" to the City when the church towers were illuminated on Wednesday, October 18th. Once again St. Ignatius became a beacon of light on the western landscape.

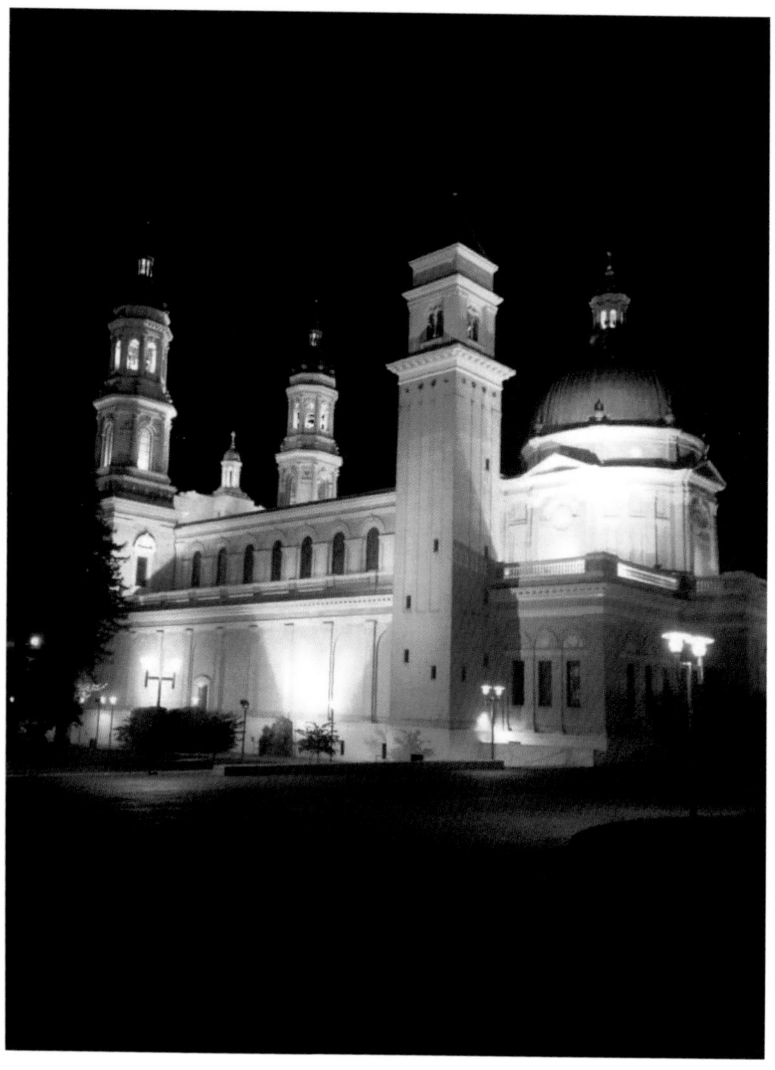

Well designed and constructed, St. Ignatius suffered minor damage, but like all public structures, it had to undergo a full inspection before services could resume– which meant the postponement of the 75th Jubilee Mass. When the original blueprints could not be located (they were buried in the University, not the Church archives), that photo of the steel frame saved the church from expensive and unnecessary retrofitting. The good news was the building was not only structurally sound, but safe.

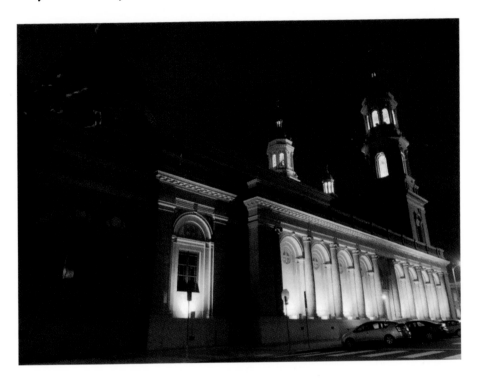

Father Gagan seized on the symbolism and made the Celebration of Light an annual event until the $400,000 "expected budget" was raised. When work commenced in 1993, the dome damage proved far more extensive than expected; the cost of reconstruction quickly doubled. While the steel frame was secure, additional supports for the marble altar and sanctuary were necessary in the former crypt area, and other deferred maintenance required attention.

THE THIRD QUAKE – THE ARCHBISHOP HAS A NEW MISSION FOR THE CHURCH – 1994

Archbishop John Quinn had a surprise in store for the Jesuits that would expand the entire scope of the restoration – in fact, more than a building restoration. When the diocese decided to study not only the church buildings after the quake, but the decreasing congregations and financial feasibility of maintaining many parish churches, ironically St. Ignatius Church was in the best condition. While St. Dominic's, Old St. Mary's, St. Francis Assisi launched major retrofit programs, St. Ignatius was well positioned to assume a new future. When the archbishop decided to close Holy Cross and St. Edward's parishes, he asked the Jesuits to assume responsibility to staff and run St. Agnes in the Haight – but most importantly, Archbishop Quinn decided to restore St. Ignatius' status as a parish -- the newest oldest Parish was born!

Chapter Eight

1994 NEWEST OLDEST PARISH IN THE DIOCESE

St. Ignatius Church was "resurrected" as a parish 132 years after Bishop Alemany took it away. The Jesuit Provincial named Father Charles Gagan, long-time San Francisco native, as the third pastor in the church's history. The new pastor created a parish council, and his first choice was 60-year daily Mass attendee Katherine Walsh, who also recruited several other Loyola Guild members and high school and college alums to join long time San Francisco families to establish a multi-year plan for the parish.

Probably the most important aspect of Father Gagan's 18-year tenure as pastor was the parish's adoption of Sacred Heart and St. Dominic's elementary schools, which then combined into the Megan Firth Academy, now Mission Dolores Academy. This became the parish's missionary outpost – to provide Catholic educations for the inner-city families who could not afford Catholic school tuitions. The SI Class of 1955 (Governor Jerry Brown's class) continues to raise scholarships for Mission Dolores Academy students to attend St. Ignatius College Prep.

Liturgical Changes: The schedule of services went through a major overhaul. Since the Carmelite Chapel already offered a 7am Mass convenient for St. Mary's Hospital doctors and nurses, the first Sunday Mass was the 8am "quiet" Mass, followed by the popular 9:30 Family Mass with contemporary music, then the last morning liturgy with classic music at 11am. When the 4pm Mass was moved to 5pm, some speculated this was another 49er Football adjustment, a Joe Montana shift – moving Mass starting time to after the televised 49er game. Regardless of the reasons, the later start time drew larger congregations.

Musical Tradition: Lay leadership teams studied the traditions and resources of the parish to set goals for St. Ignatius' 2nd Century. The parish has long been known for the quality of its liturgical music programs. Throughout its history, choirs have graced worship with a wide variety of classical, liturgical and contemporary music. The use of choral masterworks for the "high liturgies" of Advent, Christmas, Holy Week and Easter services continued to draw worshippers from throughout the Bay Area. Since the church has superb acoustics, outside music groups – especially the Chanticleer ensemble -- often booked the church for sacred concerts.

Church Art: While the church itself is a masterful work of art, the parish decided to create an internal art gallery – the Manresa Gallery. When Ignatius first experienced his vocation at Manresa, he often contemplated the mysteries of scripture through works of art. Therefore, a major Jesuit tradition has been the incorporation of art into worship and prayer. Designed by Father James Blaettler, the gallery continues to offer seasonal exhibits of contemporary devotional art for prayer and contemplation. At Christmas, the church displays its century old Nativity Scene with imported figurines that date back to the pre-1906 church. Finally, the parish recently had the stations of the cross paintings restored to pristine condition with improved lighting.

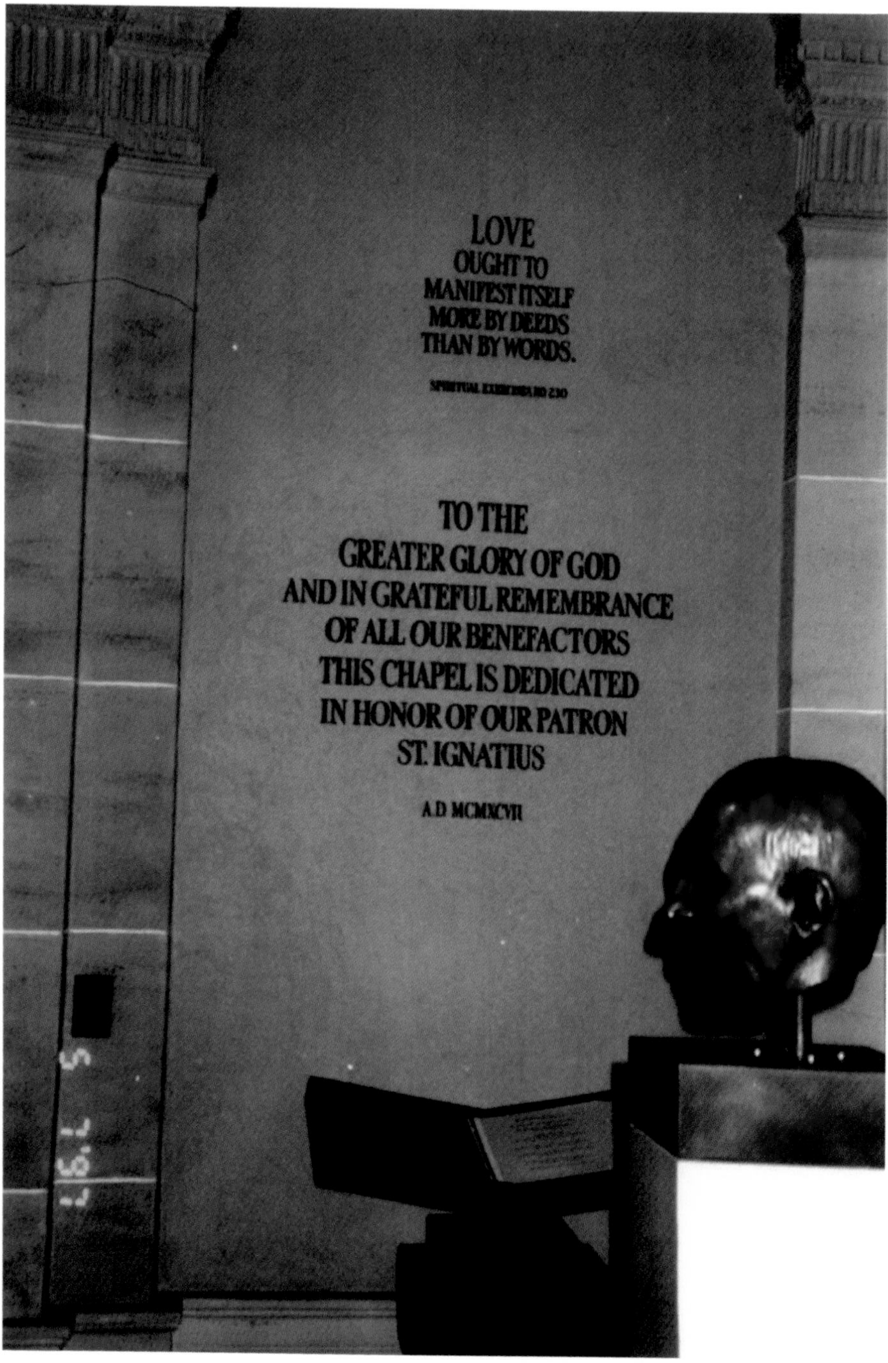
LOVE
OUGHT TO
MANIFEST ITSELF
MORE BY DEEDS
THAN BY WORDS.
TO THE
GREATER GLORY OF GOD
AND IN GRATEFUL REMEMBRANCE
OF ALL OUR BENEFACTORS
THIS CHAPEL IS DEDICATED
IN HONOR OF OUR PATRON
ST. IGNATIUS
A.D. MCMXCVII

Building Updates: First on the list of repairs to match to the handicapped entrance on Parker Street was an internal handicapped slope to the main aisle. Pews were removed to create wheelchair access. Next on the list was the conversion of the vestibule flower room into a handicapped bathroom. Even though the church survived the 1989 earthquake, the roof, the spires, the organ and various mechanical equipment were long overdue for repairs and replacement. The pastor and his team spent the first years raising the needed funds to fix the dome and cupola, install new carpeting and flooring for the aisles, and update electrical and lighting systems.

THREE IMPORTANT CHURCH CURATORS

Father Tom Lucas, SJ, an acclaimed Jesuit historian and artist, designed and directed the restoration of Ignatius Loyola's rooms at the Gesu in Rome. Father Tom designed the stained-glass window above Mary's altar, the Ignatius Loyola shrine, and the Our Lady of Guadalupe chapel; he also supervised the refurbishing of many of the side chapels and inventoried the historical vestments and church artifacts.

Fr. Jim Blaettler, SJ designed and curated exhibits in the Manresa Gallery inside the church. He also served as advisor to the parish during the capital campaign to redesign the church lighting. His use of theatrical lighting fixtures on an elaborate dimmer system has allowed church services to use light as a source of prayer and inspiration.

Ray Frost, the first parish sacristan, first attended St. Ignatius in 1974 while a student at the University of California, Berkeley. As sacristan, Ray supervised the set ups for weddings, funerals, choral concerts, graduations, and special events like the university's 150th celebration. He collaborated with parishioners to promote Eucharistic Adoration and Respect for Life ministries.

Joel Villanon, artist and designer, received national awards for his work on the Mary, Joseph and Reconciliation chapels. In 1997, he received the National AIA Design Award and a national Religious Architecture Award. A special feature of his reconciliation chapel is the wooden sculpture of the Prodigal Son.

THE FIRST AND ONLY 20TH CENTURY PASTOR

Fr. Gagan grew up across the street on Chabot Terrace, attended Mass before the installation of the marble altar, served as an altar boy at the high school. When he entered the Society of Jesus in 1955, his mother Josephine with her dry wit and wry smile bemusedly stated that young Charlie said that he would someday be pastor of St. Ignatius Church.

The parish team proposed a three-phase restoration project. The immediate need was the installation of fire safety doors and construction of a Reconciliation Chapel. Second, funds were assigned for the repairs and maintenance of the roof gutters, the bell tower, and the skylights. New flooring, new carpeting, and new lighting would modernize the major church systems. The final stage would begin repairs and restoration of the Fulton Street Towers.

When Father Gagan retired from parish duties but continued as spiritual father and fundraiser for Mission Dolores Academy, his farewell Mass was one the great parish celebrations, featuring members of the San Francisco Symphony orchestra and San Francisco Opera, with a special tented dining area on Welch Hall lawn for over 300 parishioners under the illuminated towers of the church. A set of bells was installed in the eastern steeple to commemorate his three terms (18 years) as pastor of St. Ignatius Church.

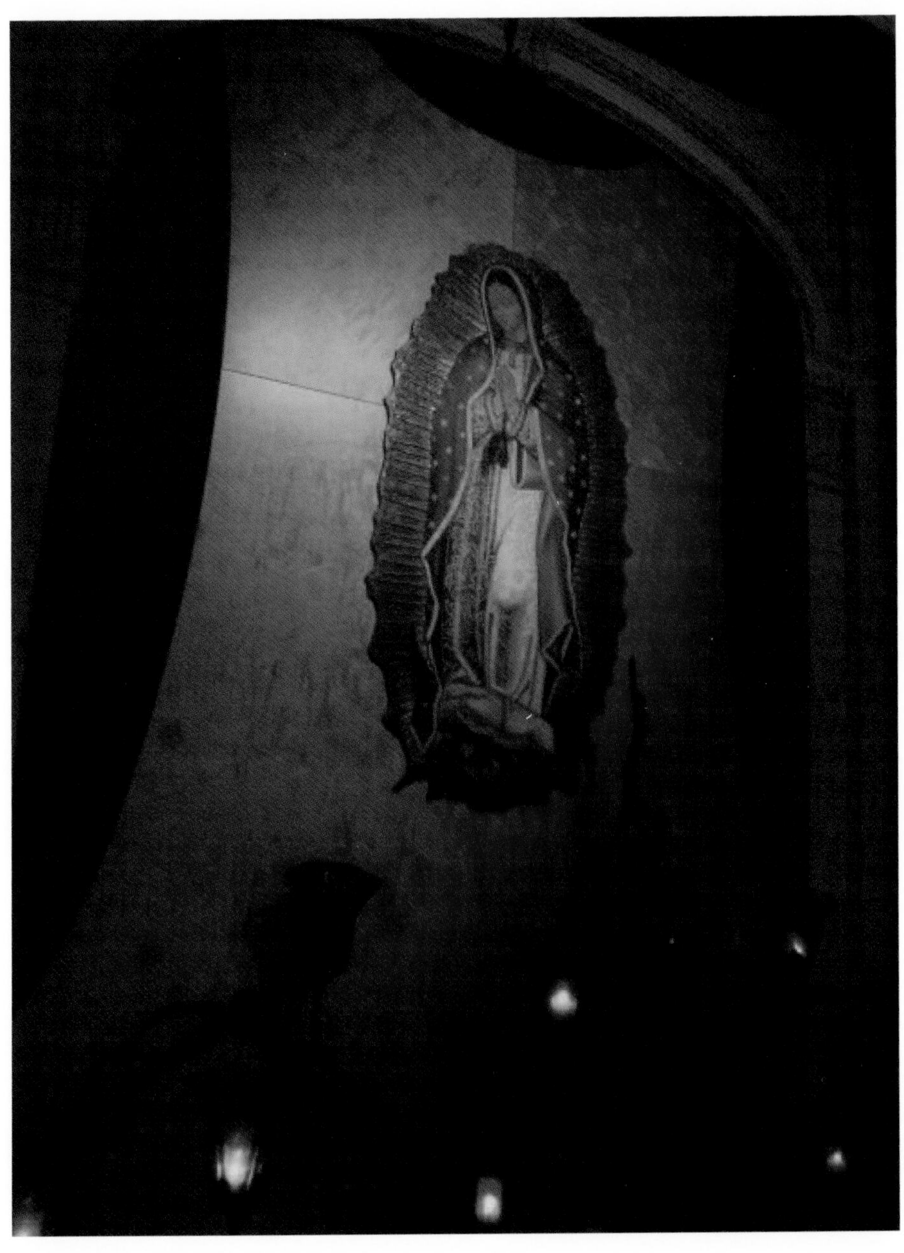

Chapter Nine

A SECOND CENTURY CENTENNIAL PARISH WITH PASSION AND COMPASSION

With the appointment of SI's 4th pastor, Father Gregory Bonfiglio, former president of Jesuit High School in Sacramento, St. Ignatius Parish began preparations for the Centennial Celebration of the dedication of the church and a second century of service. Fr. Greg engaged parishioners in a six-month process to discern a new mission statement to guide the second century mission of St. Ignatius. Following the lead from the General Congregational documents of the world-wide Society of Jesus, the parish asked this question: how do we build and sustain a living church that will inspire parishioners and the city to aspire to the greater glory of God?

Clearly, the physical building exists, but the spiritual building is always under construction, refurbishing, and rededication.

From the early days in the sand dunes on "outer" Market Street, and later to the post-earthquake and fire ruins on Van Ness, the Jesuits did more than build a church or a school. The Jesuits' first mission was always to care for the community. The Jesuits certainly provided generations with spiritual and sacramental nourishment; however, the Jesuits and their graduates also fed the city with public service in government, business, law, medicine, education – but most of all, in taking moral positions on serious social issues. For example, when the church on Market Street was being built, the Jesuits refused to use cheaper bricks made by underpaid Chinese laborers; the Jesuits objected because such a purchase would be a violation of justice. In the 1950s, both USF and St. Ignatius high school led the way with racially integrated athletic teams, often at the expense of donations and criticism. With the formation of the parish and under the leadership of Father Gagan, the community began several programs of outreach; with the formalization of a new mission statement, Father Greg and the parish team wanted to redefine how the new parish would continue the legacy of service and social action.

The Mission Statement embraces all aspects of St. Ignatius' history in San Francisco. The parish committed itself to being inclusive and inviting in greater service to family, friends and strangers:

"As companions of Jesus, the Jesuits and the parish community reaffirmed the mission of growing in our relationship with God and to find the inspiration, desire, and strength to be men and women for others. We seek to find god in all things by deepening our faith, listening with discerning and joyful hearts, and actively serving the poor and suffering, all for the greater glory of God."

THE CENTENNIAL CELEBRATION

Father Greg Bonfiglio and Father Charles Gagan, SI's living pastors, and Jesuits from all over the Jesuit province, gathered in October of 2014 to celebrate the centennial of St. Ignatius Church with parishioners and graduates of SI and USF. In anticipation of the event, the Shrines of Anthony of Padua and Ignatius Loyola in back of the church were refurbished, the Guadalupe and Ignatius shrines were completed, and the art gallery displayed historical artifacts from the church's rich history. Most important of all and building on the work done under Father Gagan, a professional assessment was undertaken to understand what is needed so that St. Ignatius Church will continue to inspire – but also aspire – to accompany the City through the 21stcentury. First, the parish focused on the stewardship of ministry, second on the stewardship of preservation. History replayed itself: after the earthquake and fire, the Jesuits ministered to the city's people first, then turned attention towards the fire threatening their church and campus.

The massive foundations of the church building support not only a landmark physical structure, but a spiritual landmark as well – a thriving community of religious and social activities in the long-standing Jesuit tradition not only in San Francisco, but around the world.

Just as the pillars of the building uphold the structure, so do the sacramental and liturgical ministerial programs. St. Ignatius has almost as many programs as it has pillars, from baptism and confirmation programs for youth and the Rite of Christian Initiation for adults, to lectors, Eucharistic ministers, greeters, ushers, hospitality hosts, and altar servers. Following in the tradition of great Jesuit preachers and teachers, the parish has an Adult Faith Formation program, a speakers' series held in the Fromm Hall Chapel that invites nationally renowned speakers to educate and inspire parishioners on faith-based topics such as Ignatian Spirituality and social justice issues, as well as broader topics, such as advanced care directives and teen use of media and the internet..

In addition to the tradition of great choir singing at the 9:30 and 11am Sunday Masses, under Father Greg, the parish has become host to many major singing groups, some local, many national and international, including choirs from Notre Dame, Holy Cross, Boston College and other major universities, as well as Cappella Romana (Portland) and Libera (London). For many years St. Ignatius Church with its excellent acoustics has played host for Chanticleer, the world's reigning male singing ensemble who have won several Grammy Awards. In October 2018, the parish hosted the San Francisco Gay Men's Chorus for their 40th Anniversary concert. In recent years the parish has hosted the combined choirs and orchestra of St. Ignatius College Prep, USF and the parish's own singing group for the annual All Souls Liturgy on the first Sunday of November.

The arches that adorn and uphold the ceiling are the many lay leadership programs. Throughout the year, the parish hosts special annual events that celebrate and foster community – the Christmas Emporium, the Easter Egg Hunt, the Fall Parish Picnic, the Men's and Women's Retreats, and the Liturgical Planning Committee, which thoughtfully plans the decorations for Christmas, Holy Week and the Easter season. Created for the 2015-2016 Year of Mercy, 14 banners with the Corporal and Spiritual Works of Mercy hang from the columns during Lent, and a large wreath suspended from the ceiling at the transept announces Advent and is joined at Christmas by wreaths suspended from the garland-wrapped columns, and vines of spring flowers wind down those same columns during Easter, all in tribute to the great decorations of the Van Ness church, another reaching out to the past to inspire the present.

Some of the great Jesuit saints who are commemorated in the side altar shrines live in the parish outreach programs: the Neighbor to Neighbor program, which connects parishioners in need with parishioners who help: meals to new parents, rides to doctor appointment for elderly or infirm, Eucharist to homebound and those in convalescent homes, and more. In 2017 the parish revitalized the old bookstore in the church sacristy and opened the Shop at St. Ignatius, offering a wide selection of spiritual and theological reading materials, Confirmation and First Communion gifts, and other religious goods.

As the stained-glass windows of Christ, Mary, and the Saints look out over the city of San Francisco, so the parish's numerous social programs look out to serve its people. Some provide food and nourishment, such as the Sandwich Saturday, Simple Needs Sunday, Brown Bag Sunday, and the Shelter Meal programs. Some provide social advocacy and support, such as the Solidarity Network, which advocates for immigration reform and provides accompaniment to refugee families, and the Advocacy Committee, which advocates for victims of human trafficking, and the Gabriel Project for women facing crisis pregnancies without family assistance. A throw-back to Father Nobli's work with San Quentin in the 1860s, the parish co-sponsors Get on the Bus program, which helps to maintain connections between children and their incarcerated parents. The parish also actively participates in the Gubbio Project in the Tenderloin and Habitat for Humanity.

The Stations of the Cross find representation in the parish's international outreach. St. Ignatius Parish entered into a covenantal relationship with Parroquia San Antonio in Soyapango, El Salvador. Known as Las Vecinas de El Salvador delegations from the sister parishes regularly visit one another, deepening our bonds of friendship and solidarity and working together in support of peace with justice.

SPIRES THAT ASPIRE TO INSPIRE – SAVING ST IGNATIUS CHURCH – BACK TO THE FUTURE

As Elsie Robinson wrote back in 1914, the twin spires of St. Ignatius Church inspire the people of San Francisco – a call to worship, gratitude, and stewardship. The University and the City both chose a phoenix rising from the ashes to new life because the mythical bird captures that pioneer spirit of the city after the earthquake and fire in 1906 – San Franciscans rebuild and preserve our history and heritage, so those same towers inspire the San Francisco community to care for the preservation of this magnificent church.

As the church enters its second hundred years, the twin spires that nightly light the city's Western skies recapture the aspirations of generations back to the gold rush. Since 1851, San Francisco's Jesuits have always been reaching up and reaching out, bringing hope and joy, offering inspiration and consolation to the world class city on the Pacific Rim. During the wars those towers were most sailors final sight of the continental United States; those same towers were the first sight of their homeland when they returned. For generations of immigrants, the twin towers welcomed and embraced the weary traveler. How proud the early Jesuits would be to know that St. Ignatius Church is the first significant landmark before sailing under the Golden Gate. Because of the fog, the salt air, the wind and the rain, the spires are in constant need of refurbishing and repairs after over a century of service.

Under the leadership of Father Greg Bonfiglio, a number of studies have been conducted to assess the condition and safety of the church building. They determined three major – and imminent – projects were needed to preserve the integrity of St. Ignatius Church for the future.

First – and perhaps most important -- the Spires, dome and campanile, visual landmarks and together a symbol of the city -- have survived wind, rain, fog and earthquakes, including the 1989 Loma Prieta jolt. However, major portions of those building elements need immediate replacement of their 105-year-old cladding to protect their structural integrity.

Second, the 125 windows in the church are in need of various repairs. Half of the windows are stained glass and have an average age of 70 years out of 120 years. While minor repairs were made in 1994, broken panes, deteriorated lead and wood frames and more are in desperate need of major repair.

Third, the exterior lighting, installed for the 75th anniversary of the church's dedication, is in a state of failure. A new design that uses current LED technology and is more environmentally friendly is near completion to return the church to its nighttime prominence on the City's skyline.

Fourth, after more than a century of welcoming students, parishioners and pilgrims alike, some of the pews need repair and all need refinishing, and the kneelers need to be replaced with a period design and modern hardware.

Fifth, our beloved church welcomes friends and strangers alike with its doors open daily from 6:00 a.m. to 6:30 p.m. For the safety of all and the protection of this spiritual and architectural treasure, plans are in the works to install a fire alarm system for the first time in its history.

Finally, the existing roof is nearing the end of its lifespan. While rain no longer falls on congregants in the pews, and the rain-catching flower pots and buckets are no longer needed, the risk to the overall integrity of the building is too high to forgo a new roof at this time.

The second century begins much as the first century with the Save St. Ignatius campaign, but actually returns St. Ignatius Church to the days of Father Maraschi – a need to raise funds to protect the work of Ignatius and his followers and those San Franciscans inspired by the vision. The Jesuit Fathers have always taken big risks in San Francisco – building in outer sand of St. Ann's valley, then in the Van Ness sand dunes– only to have an earthquake and fire point the way out of the valleys to the hilltop. Now St. Ignatius represents the dreams generations that have gone before, the faith and generosity of the present generation, and the aspirations and inspirations of the generations to come – for the greater glory of God. AMDG

APPENDIX OF MINISTRIES

SACRAMENTAL AND LITURGICAL PROGRAMS:

Rite of Christian Initiation for Adults (RCIA) is for those wishing to be baptized as Catholics, or Christians who would like to join the Catholic community, for Catholics seeking preparation for First Communion or Confirmation, or Catholics returning after a long absence.

Eucharistic Ministers are parishioners who volunteer to administer the Sacrament of the Holy Eucharist and help the priest distribute the Body and Blood of Christ at Mass.

Hospitality Hosts, Greeters, Ushers The parish sponsors many hospitality events structured for parishioners to get to know each other, or serve as greeters or ushers at 9:30 am 11:00 am and 5pm Sunday Masses.

Music Ministry & Choirs the 5pm Liturgical Choir is open to new members. Rehearsal is typically 30 – 45 minutes before mass begins.

Singers assist the congregation in worship by leading the singing during Mass. Instrumentalists enrich and add varied accompaniment to our sung prayer. Special opportunities exist for adults and children in the Christmas Choir, as well as the opportunity to perform a classic choral work at the annual Requiem Mass in November.

Liturgical Planning and Environment (LPEC) plans major liturgical events celebrated throughout the liturgical year. The committee meets once a month, or as-needed, based on the liturgical season. In addition to decorating the church for the Advent, Christmas, Lenten and Easter seasons, parishioners to provide sewing, carpentry, design, as well as cleaning up and storing of seasonal decorations.

Lectors nourish the faith of believers by proclaiming audible and intelligible language the Scripture passages for the Liturgy of the Word during a mass. Lectors participate in the Mass by reading one of the designated readings or the Prayers of Petition.

Acolytes/Altar Servers Altar Servers, Acolytes assist the priest in the celebration of the Eucharist during Mass in the Sanctuary.

The Spiritual Exercises of St. Ignatius/ 19th Annotation retreat With one of the Jesuit fathers, or trained lay directors, parishioners can experience St. Ignatius' Spiritual Exercises where they work through the meditations of the four weeks of the spiritual exercises while living their normal daily life. Usually the retreat involves one hour of meditation a day and periodical meetings with the spiritual director to savor the insights and graces of the experience.

Guided Ignatian Meditations led by one of the Jesuit priests allow the faithful to "Find God in all things." These are usually held after the Saturday evening 5pm Masses.

Catechists for Children's Faith Formation (CFF) Children's Faith Forma on (CFF) offers classes to assist parents in helping their children (3 years to grade 8) grow more aware of God, their own relationship with Jesus, and to learn and understand Catholic belief, prayers, and identity.

Children's Liturgy of the Word (CLOW) During the 9:30 am Sunday liturgy, children from Kindergarten through Grade 4 are invited to meet separately to hear and reflect upon an age-appropriate version of the Sunday Gospel, especially designed to make the Gospel message relevant to the lives and experiences of young children.

Confirmation In the Archdiocese of San Francisco, the Youth Confirmation Program is a two-year process. At St. Ignatius, the process begins in the 7th grade. We do require that participants are registered, active members of the parish. Classes begin at the start of the school year in September.

PARISH COMMUNITY GROUPS

Communications Strategy Team assists with development of the overall parish strategy and with setting priorities for internal communications to parishioners; and for external communications to engage potential new parishioners and invite greater participation in parish life.

Church Building and Preservation Committee advises the pastor and staff by soliciting and reviewing proposals for the long-term maintenance, preservation, and enhancement of the historic church building, its infrastructure, and systems. It recommends which firms or contractors to engage, advises on the sequencing and structuring of the work, discusses design considerations, and aligns building plans with the capital budget.

St. Ignatius in the Neighborhood Several times throughout the year, our parishioners graciously open their homes to neighboring parishioners to create a more intimate opportunity for us to get to know our fellow parishioners. Light food and wine are usually served.

Adult Faith Formation (AFF) Speaker Series The AFF Speaker Series provides opportunities for adults to nurture their faith, including a renowned speaker series on Sunday mornings after the 9:30 am Mass.

Men's & Women's Retreats a half day event held in late October, is a special time for reflection and discussion on the meaning of the Word in the daily lives of men in our contemporary, pluralistic society.

Parish Picnic (Annual) is held each September at a combined 10am Sunday Mass (9:30 am & 11:00 am Masses combined) outside the church on the USF lawn for a BBQ lunch, silent auction, raffle, and fun & games for 300+ families.

Christmas Emporium one Sunday in December, the parish invites vendors from around the Bay Area to join us for a day of shopping and holiday fun, a way to do some Christmas shopping as well as mingle with other parishioners. Santa even visits!

Advent Giving Tree St. Ignatius Parish supports children, teens, adults, and seniors in need through the Advent Giving Tree Project.

Easter Egg Hunt is always a great community event attracting over 400 parishioners, both young and old. The hunt begins following the 9:30 am Mass on Easter Sunday. With over 160 pounds of candy stuffed into 1,800 Easter eggs, no one leaves empty-handed. The Easter Bunny generally pays a visit.

Neighbor to Neighbor are parish volunteers who work together to periodically assist other parishioners in need, like driving an elderly parishioner to a doctor's appointment, help with grocery shopping, or bring the Eucharist.

SOCIAL JUSTICE OUTREACH ACTIVITIES:

St. Ignatius Advocacy Committee aims to influence decisions with social, economic, and political systems and institutions. It is distinct from direct service in that it seeks to address the root cause of social injustice. After a series of talks on the issues of immigration, ecological justice, human trafficking, environmental justice, and restorative justice, parishioners were invited in 2015 to participate in a discernment process to choose a justice issue to address for the parish. The two issues that surfaced were Sanctuary and Human Trafficking.

Sandwich Saturdays On the first Saturday of every month, volunteers gather in the former Xavier Hall (now Fromm Hall) kitchen to make 700 sandwiches for the homeless. Since `1994, these volunteers have made over 63,000 sandwiches, a miracle of loaves and fishes proportions.

Brown Bag Lunch is a year-round outreach program aimed at helping to feed the hungry, by providing homemade sack lunches donated by parishioners each month. On the *next to last* weekend of each month, empty lunch bags are distributed at the church entrances. The *following* weekend, homemade lunches consisting of a sandwich, fruit, cookies and a snack are deposited in the baskets at the entrances of the church at all weekend Masses.

Shelter Meal Program serves San Francisco residents in need solely through the work of parish volunteers who prepare hot meals in the former Xavier Hall (now Fromm Hall) kitchen two weekends a month for the homeless, or those without permanent shelter, or in need of assistance.

St. Agnes Pantry Food Drive Parishioners are invited to bring nonperishable food items to all weekend Masses on the third Sunday of the month to support local food pantries.

Simple Needs Sundays are regular Parish collection drives in support of the most basic and urgent needs of our homeless and struggling neighbors. Essential everyday items that are in constant need and short supply on the streets, like: toiletries, socks and underwear, or a warm jacket and cap in the winter, are collected on a rotating basis at Masses on the second Sunday of most months.

Get on the Bus (April-June) provides children and their caregivers with pre-trip assistance, including: prison visitation requirements, transportation, meals, travel bags, a family photograph, special activities with their parent inside, dinner, and opportunities for counseling. Due to the travel distance and distressed circumstances, this visit is often the only me most of the children will see their parents during the year. In 2015, Get on the Bus facilitated the clearances of more than 3,000 individuals to visit mothers and fathers, with approximately 1,500 children and their care-givers, and visited 11 prisons.

Parish Solidarity Network aims to raise awareness around the issues immigrant and refugee members of our community face, explore how society can be er respond to those issues, and provide support to immigrants and refugees need- ing assistance.

Habitat for Humanity (Spring & Fall) The Parish organizes Habitat "Build Days" twice a year (usually a Saturday in April and in October) and gather volunteers to help construct new housing locally.

Gubbio Project The fourth Friday of every month at 6:30 AM, parishioners of St. Ignatius Parish prepare, serve, and share breakfast with homeless men and women at St. John the Evangelist Church in the Mission District.

Nursing and Convalescent Home Ministry volunteers visit with the residents of Hayes Convalescent Hospital, one block from Alamo Square.

Star Community works with SF Archdiocese to provide families a safe place to live while developing a plan to secure stability and housing. Families typically arrive at Star Community Home in crisis; homeless, fearful, hungry, lonely, desperate, and penniless. The home immediately offers a safe place to live by providing nutritious meals and help build the skills necessary for a self-sufficient future. Families exit Star with housing, a stable source of income, and the skills they need to establish permanent exits from homelessness. Single-parent family housing stabilization success rate: 97%.

Las Vecinas de El Salvador is a social ministries Program that works to maintain an on- going relationship with the people of El Salvador through our sister parish of San Antonio in Soyapango. As sister parishes, San Antonio Parish and SI parish are committed to strengthening our friendship and working together in support of peace with justice.

Respect Life is a part of the Respect Life Program of the Archdiocese of San Francisco, formed to implement the Pastoral Plan for Pro-Life Activities of the National Conference of Catholic Bishops.

Gabriel Project Many mothers faced with crisis pregnancies feel abandoned by their families, the fathers of their babies, and their communities. Churches and pro-life service groups have sought ways to expand their embrace of women in crisis pregnancies. The Gabriel Project is a Catholic parish-based ministry conducted under the direction of the Archdiocese of San Francisco.

Senior Ministry invites seniors (50+) to come and enjoy each other's company; activities include movies, meals and prayer and meets once a month, on the second Friday of the month.

ABOUT THE AUTHOR

Peter Devine, a 5th generation San Franciscan, has taught at St. Ignatius College Prep for 46 years. His great grandfather attended St. Ignatius in 1868 on Market Street, his great uncle attended on Van Ness Avenue, and his father served Mass at both the "shirt factory" and the current SI church. As Drama Director Peter received recognition as "inspirational teacher" at the 2015 Tony Awards from Darren Criss, Adam Jacobs and Bart Sher and has also received awards from President Clinton, and Stanford, Santa Clara and Northwestern universities, and the National Foundation for the Arts.